CONFERENCE OF DEFENCE ASS

ANNUAL SEMINAR

JANUARY 1992

LEANER AND MEANER:

ARMED FORCES IN THE POST GULF WAR ERA

iii

The Conference of Defence Associations Institute
President, Colonel Ben Shapiro
Executive Director, David E. Code

The Conference of Defence Associations Institute (CDAI) is a non-profit enterprise dedicated to promoting a better understanding of Canada's national defence and security. Although the creation of the Institute was encouraged by many defence officials, the CDA Institute is an independent operation with its own set of objectives:

- Conducting research and analysis into current defence needs and priorities
- Stimulating discussion and debate on Canada's defence structure and policy
- Promoting knowledge, respect and understanding of Canadian military history
- Contributing to a better understanding of national defence through public information services

The CDA Institute is dedicated to the creation of a dynamic programme of information and education, responsive and open for membership to all Canadians. All donations to the Institute are tax deductible and donors are placed on the mailing list for all CDAI publications:

- FORUM magazine — one of Canada's leading defence journals, mailed four times per year
- CDAI Newsline — the Institute's quarterly newsletter
- All book publications — recent titles include:

  They Stand on Guard: A Defence Direction for Canada
  by Bob Hicks, M.P.
  Canada's Militia: A Heritage at Risk
  by Professor T.C. Willett
  Peacemaking: Canada's Role
  (1991 Seminar Proceedings) edited by W.J. Yost and Thomas St. Denis

For more information about the CDA Institute and its activities please contact:

The CDA Institute
Suite 601, 100 Gloucester Street
Ottawa, Ontario, K2P 0A4

Tel: (613) 563-1387 Fax: (613) 235-0784

LEANER AND MEANER:

ARMED FORCES IN THE POST GULF WAR ERA

Edited by:

David E. Code and Caroline Ursulak

The Conference of Defence Associations Institute

Published by the
Conference of Defence Associations Institute
601 — 100 Gloucester Street
Ottawa, Ontario
K2P 0A4

Cover: Canadian Forces.

The CDA Institute gratefully acknowledges the assistance of
the **Canadian Institute for International Peace and Security,**
whose grant helped to make this publication possible. The views
expressed in this book are those of the speakers only and do
not necessarily reflect the views of either the Canadian Institute
for International Peace and Security or the Conference of
Defence Associations Institute.

ISBN: 0-921687-09-5

CONTENTS

PAGE

PREFACE   Brigadier General W.J. Yost   ix

PART I   **SEMINAR PROCEEDINGS**

I   **Introduction**   1
Bernard Wood

II   **Changes in the Canadian Armed Forces**   7
General A.J.G.D. de Chastelain

III   **Police and Military Cooperation in Canada**   31
Assistant Commissioner Michel Thivierge

IV   **The Future of Arms Control**   47
Brigadier General B.A. Goetze

V   **Progress in Making a Total Force**   63
Lieutenant General J.C. Gervais

VI   **The United Nations as a Peacemaker**   77
L. Yves Fortier

PART II   **CDA ANNUAL GENERAL MEETING PROCEEDINGS**

VII   **Canadian Defence Policy and the International Strategic Environment**   93
The Honourable Marcel Masse

VIII   **1991 in Review**   103
General A.J.G.D. de Chastelain

IX   **Strategic Planning and Other Reserve Issues**   119
Major General F.A.J. Mariage

PARTICIPANTS

Honourable Marcel Masse, P.C., M.P.,
Minister of National Defence

General A.J.G.D. de Chastelain, CMM, CD
Chief of the Defence Staff

Lieutenant General J.C. Gervais, CMM, CD
Commander, Mobile Command

Major General F.A.J. Mariage, CD
Chief of Reserves and Cadets

Brigadier General B.A. Goetze, OMM, CD, Ph.D
Director General, International Policy Operations

Brigadier General D.A. Pryer, CD
Chairman, Conference of Defence Associations

Colonel B. Shapiro, CD
President, Conference of Defence Associations Institute

Assistant Commissioner J.W.M. Thivierge
Commanding Officer "A" Division, RCMP

L. Yves Fortier, C.C., Q.C., B.A., B.C.L., B.Litt (OXON), LL.D.(Hon)
Former Canadian Ambassador to the United Nations

Bernard Wood
Chief Executive Officer,
Canadian Institute for International Peace and Security

Moderator

Colonel His Honour Judge Ronald A. Jacobson, C.D.
Colonel Commandant,
The Royal Regiment of Canadian Artillery

PREFACE

by
Brigadier General (Ret) William J. Yost

February 24, 1992

On September 17, 1991 the Minister of National Defence unveiled a revised Defence Policy for Canada to meet changes in the rapidly shifting international and domestic scene. The Minister outlined how the Regular Forces would become "leaner" by cutting back from 84,000 to 76,000 personnel. This reduction in numbers would be offset by increasing the size of the Reserves. Improved training of Reservists would be achieved by the "Total Force" concept — integrating Regular and Reserve troops in units. A new capital equipment funding target of 30 percent of the budget was set to improve their equipment to a level needed for modern warfare.

Overall, the intent seemed to be to follow the example set by the United States and other allies following the Gulf War. Their stated goal was to make their forces smaller without losing their punch — to a large measure relying on the new sophisticated weapons proven in battle against the Iraqis. This process has given rise to the term "Leaner and Meaner" — which was adopted as the theme of the Conference of Defence Associations Institute's annual Seminar on January 23, 1992.

The seminar speakers examined the structure and tasks of the Canadian Forces provided in the new Defence Policy statement, in an attempt to define problems which must be addressed. Changes in United Nations attitudes, with the likelihood of increased attention to enforcement operations and peacemaking activities, as opposed to purely peacekeeping, were outlined; along with disarmament and treaty regulation activities and police/ military cooperation.

I was left with considerable misgivings at the end of the two days of addresses recorded in this book. With the reduction of our Forces in Germany already underway, cutbacks in recruiting levels, and the Force Reduction Program released in January 1992 by ADM (Personnel), there was no doubt that the Regular Forces were becoming "leaner". But would these smaller Regular Forces be augmented by a sufficiently well-trained and larger Reserve Force to maintain current commitments? And would the new equipment to make them "meaner" on the battlefield really be procured?

Various equipping programs have been cancelled in this past year and others put on hold. It is obvious that the Department does not have the money, after the cutbacks in the 1989 and 1990 Budgets, to continue with even the fairly modest equipping program which had been previously approved. The Militia have not been given the funding necessary to carry out training at an improved tempo, or to proceed with recruiting. I really cannot see a great improvement in the equipment or training proficiency of the Reserves, although we have been pursuing a Total Force approach for many months. It all boils down to resources — DND has not been able to assign the funding to Total Force enhancement needed to match the rhetoric. Money saved from personnel cuts is obviously going to equipping, but the massive savings from closing Lahr and Baden have yet to be realized. The government has been unwilling, for political reasons, to implement even the most obvious of the infrastructure changes involving Base closures in Canada. While the size of the Forces dwindles, their equipment funding is also faltering.

The Minister, in his remarks on January 24, 1992 was very positive, concluding with "The Canadian Forces *will* have the means to implement the defence policy I announced in September.

They will be leaner, to be sure, but they will be better equipped and able to carry out all their missions with the skill and professionalism for which they are known". With these background thoughts, I set my pen aside to await the federal Government's February 25, 1992 Budget statement.

February 26, 1992

The DND Budget is always vulnerable because Canadians do not feel strongly about Defence in peacetime, and there are vociferous anti-military lobbies who would like to see our Forces disappear. They may get their wish if the current trend continues, and we will end up with only para-military forces.

The previous two Federal Budgets had seriously slashed Defence funding, in spite of the equipment problems which were highlighted during the Gulf War. In the Budget of February 25, 1992 it was announced that the withdrawal of forces and close out of Lahr and Baden would be accelerated by a year, and all the troops would return. The plan to leave 1,100 troops in Europe was cancelled, and the strength of the Armed Forces would be cut to a new target of 75,000 over the next three years.

From a financial standpoint the Department has not suffered too heavy a blow. DND must trim $258 million from this year's spending and over the next five years $2.2 billion will be trimmed from the *projected budget*. In terms of money, however, the Department's budget will actually increase from 12.1 billion in FY 1991/92 to 12.3 billion next year and 12.7 billion in FY 1993/94.

Mr. Masse has been quoted as saying the cuts are not a serious problem. "Nothing has been affected in terms of investments, the big equipment that we need," he added. That seems to be the case, and perhaps with the country's economy in crisis we should consider DND to have escaped with relatively minor cuts. Certainly we can live with the cancellation of the 1,100 man Standing Task Force in Europe. We had proposed this to the Standing Committee on National Defence and Veterans Affairs at a recent briefing but recommended Canada maintain an airhead at a UK air base to support our NATO, UN, and humanitarian activities in Europe, the Middle East and Africa. With a strength of 100 to 300 military it would also serve as a Canadian token military force in Europe for NATO purposes. A forward base will be needed to support our ongoing activities, and while it is not as glamorous sounding as the 1,100 man strike force, it is far more necessary.

I suppose the most worrisome effects of all this came from the realization that you don't get more defence for less money, and we are getting very close to the point where general purpose forces will no longer be feasible within the budget restraints. In addition, once again a new budget has forced important changes in a Defence Policy which was approved by Cabinet only four months ago. How can we plan ahead with this uncertainty?

Our armed forces are becoming leaner, and the February budget accelerated this process, but the evidence seems to point to weaker, not meaner, forces in the future.

W.J. Yost BGen (Ret)
Vice President
CDA Institute

I

Introduction

by
Bernard Wood,
Chief Executive Officer
Canadian Institute for International Peace and Security

It is a pleasure to be able to share a few thoughts with the CDA annual seminar participants at the start of your very timely discussion on armed forces after the Gulf War, and of course after the Cold War.

The Canadian Institute for International Peace and Security is responsible for promoting knowledge and understanding of questions relating to international peace and security, from a Canadian point of view. According to the mandate that we have been given by parliament, we collaborate and support many different organizations and activities across the country, including the Conference of Defence Associations.

In the past it was sometimes difficult, particularly in the context of the Cold War, to encourage constructive and reasoned dialogue between the different conceptions of peace and security in our society. It isn't surprising that these objectives, which are among the most fundamental for all of humanity, generated profound differences and passionate debate. I have always considered that, by establishing such an agency, our parliament had envisaged and hoped that we would be an oasis of objective analysis in the eye of the storm.

The Cold War was obviously the greatest armed confrontation in history. In retrospect, it mercifully proved to be a fairly stable security relationship, although it was ruinously costly to the treasuries of the main protagonists, and often in blood to Third World countries drawn into shooting wars where East-West rivalries often played a significant part.

In the past couple of years, as it became clear that the Cold War was ending, some people with little sense of history asked if this meant that the Canadian Institute for International Peace and Security could now close up shop. I never hesitated for a moment in my conviction that the end of the Cold War meant precisely the opposite. The film of history has not ended, it has started running again, at full speed, after the prolonged freeze-frame of global superpower confrontation was unlocked. As Dickens said of another revolutionary era, these are some of the best of times, and the worst of times. The period now upon us is filled with promise and peril, and the decisions and actions taken in the coming months and years will have decisive impacts on the peace and security of our species and of all the others on this planet.

I am convinced that there is far more scope for a country like ours, and its citizens, to now influence the course of events than there was in a world so dominated by two gigantic military adversaries. By the same token, there is more need for a country like ours, and its citizens, to carry commensurate shares of the responsibility in the world.

Soldiers have always known that many of the basic challenges to peace and security, and the instruments for handling them, are non-military in character. This is more true than ever in a world of tighter interdependence, expanded communications, and apocalyptic military technologies. We now have a long and urgent list of underlying security issues to address.

Military force, and even the threat of military force, already has a dramatically reduced role in many parts of the world and in many international relationships. Perhaps most notably within Western Europe, after North America, we have seen the emergence of what Karl Deutsch called "security communities" among states which no longer expect or fear the use of force in relations between them.

It was always the height of ethnocentric arrogance in past decades for North Americans to think they could make a contribution to European peace and security by going over and preaching on the spirit of our long undefended border. It would now be the height of arrogance, and imprudence, because of the end of the Cold War, to assume away the continuing dangers of the use of organized violence in future relations with what was the Soviet Union, within and across frontiers in Europe and elsewhere in the world, and even within our own blessed but still imperfect society.

Leaving aside that last, internal, dimension, it can even be argued that the breakdown of an organized, global balance of nuclear terror may have made military force *more* usable, rather than less, in human affairs; and other trends may also compound the temptation.

If any proof had been needed for these sober conclusions, it was provided by Saddam Hussein's invasion of Kuwait, and the world's response, which came in full force a year ago. We should be careful in extracting "lessons" from that second Gulf conflict, preceded as it was by another long and bloody war, also launched by Iraqi aggression, and fed by exports of weapons rather than reversed by UN action.

I fear that different leaders, and different nations, may have taken away very different "lessons". Perhaps the most important question for your topic today is whether more governments took away the message that the threat of modern conventional warfare requires them to devote much *greater* resources to arming themselves adequately for it, or on the other hand that it is simply too advanced, expensive and dangerous a game for them to play, and thus that they should abandon arms races and find other paths to security. The evidence so far is probably mixed, with only a few states increasing their military spending, but a dangerous flood of former Soviet arms on the market, and others still too ready, as well, to ply this trade into regions of potential conflict.

Some took away the hope, or fear, that henceforth the United States, as the sole superpower, would be ready, willing, and able to serve as the world's policeman in every conflict. In my opinion, they are gravely mistaken. Even if it were possible for Washington to rally and lead a UN-authorized posse to respond to every military crisis, it would be undesirable and quickly unsustainable. The invasion of Kuwait was an extraordinarily clear and blatant case of interstate aggression, in a region of vital interest, and even there the achievement of a fully multilateral response was a close-run thing.

We are going to need better-prepared, and more genuinely multilaterally directed and controlled, forces in readiness for other peace-enforcement actions, as well as for a much heavier volume of peacekeeping activity. For some time to come, the world is still going to need powerful Western military forces and alliances to guard against other risks and potential threats that cannot yet be handled by the United Nations, and some of which cannot yet even be predicted. As Desmond Morton pointed out in a now famous article in our Institute's magazine, military planning is plagued by the contradictory need to prepare for the unpredictable. Probably the only thing worse than the often misdirected efforts to prepare would be to make none at all.

NATO may not yet have changed enough to respond to the changed circumstances, but it has already changed more than most of its critics thought possible. Significantly, hardly anyone is now calling for its dissolution, least of all its former adversaries in Central and Eastern Europe, who now see it as a rare and valued pole of stability in a much more unstable and unpredictable world.

Where does all this leave Canada and its armed forces? This is surely a dominant question for your deliberations today. The Government produced an overdue statement of its general directions in September 1991, in a step which I hope will firmly entrench the practice of annual updates to revise the defence appreciation, make course corrections as necessary, and manage major spending programs on a rolling basis.

I would like to raise one or two final provocative questions of possible interest in your discussions today. First, as one who sometimes has to think up catchy titles himself, I still wonder whether your organizers might have resisted the temptation to rhyme, with the "leaner and meaner" view of armed forces in the post Gulf War era. There is no question that armed forces are going to *leaner* in most countries because of stringent budgetary discipline.

State of the art fighting forces are obviously also going to be *meaner* in the sense of being literally more deadly accurate through the effective use of high technology intelligence, command, control, communications and weapons systems and counter-systems. The Gulf War did show how the targeting capability of modern armed forces can focus their destructive power to the point of blurring the distinction between so-called "conventional" and "unconventional" weapons. Even in some of their non-fighting roles, such as peacekeeping, or search and rescue support, modern armed forces should be able to greatly improve their effectiveness through high technology systems in areas other than offensive weapons. The fighting arms which any country feels that it needs, it will naturally want to equip with the most effective systems and counter-systems possible. I do not envisage "kinder and gentler" armed forces which is, and always will be, a contradiction in terms.

The danger in the "meaner" formulation, however, is the possible implication that the world, and individual countries, must now be moving to an overall increase in their destructive military power. My own view is the opposite, that we are in a rare moment when military strength can and must be reduced on a balanced and verified basis without prejudicing security, but in fact enhancing it. General Goetze will be outlining some of the further prospects for arms reductions in his comments. Even some of the *qualitative* strengthening of armed forces may be restrainable in ways that will save resources and maintain security.

I also believe, assuming that the overall reduction of military strength and confrontation is going to continue, that it may be time for countries like ours and those of our allies to move toward more specialized military functions and capabilities, rather than all trying to support such a wide range of military roles. In practice, this is how things worked out in the Gulf coalition: although the division of labour was probably not full satisfactory to anyone, the *principle* of a division of labour and military specialization is now increasingly inescapable for all but the very largest military powers. This will be essential to both the leanness and their effectiveness.

Just as politicians hate to talk about rationalizing defence infrastructure (the euphemism for closing redundant bases) so the various branches of our soldiers, sailors, and aviators hate to talk about rationalizing and specializing our military capabilities, because somebody's ox must inevitably get gored. My own conviction is that a country like Canada must and can find appropriate niches in all areas of international life, including the military, as well as covering our own basic requirements. In fact we already have world leadership in a couple of leading growth sectors, namely peacekeeping and verification, which I believe stand the armed forces in this country in much better stead with our public than in almost any other country I can think of. We could probably hone those specializations and aspire to one or two more alongside our modest general purpose requirements. I would like to see the defence support and strategic studies communities seriously involved in the debate on choices like these, or I fear that the choices will be made by default on the basis of blind austerity and political expediency.

II

Changes in the
Canadian Armed Forces

by
General A.J.G.D. de Chastelain
Chief of the Defence Staff

Let me thank you for the opportunity of talking to you this morning. It's a pleasure to be here and to see such a wide audience: members of the diplomatic community and the Canadian Forces as well as those of the CDA.

I have been doing a lot of talking in many places recently and few people here have not heard me speak on aspects of the new defence policy or where I think we are going. For those who heard me at the University of Calgary two days ago, or at the RCMI the week before, or at the Toronto Board of Trade, or with the Legion in New Brunswick, and who don't hear today what I said then, we'll discuss it later. It doesn't mean I have changed my mind.

Tomorrow, I will present the annual review of what we did in 1991. I will use a prepared text because, like you, my hindsight is 20/20 but my forecasting is probably zero. As Bernard Wood said and as Desmond Morton has indicated, predicting the unpredictable is a black art.

We have fought two wars in this half century, one fairly long and bloody, the other shorter and, at least from a Canadian viewpoint, not bloody. Neither was a war we had planned to fight and I suspect that's going to be the case in the future. All this by way of saying I'm not going to work from my prepared text today. I will refer to headings I have jotted down in the hope that I can touch on aspects you might find useful in this very interesting topic you are considering.

Now my staff gets very nervous when I don't speak from a prepared text because they don't know what I'm going to say. They are not alone, because I don't know what I'm going to say either. On a number of past occasions that has got me or somebody else into trouble.

Indeed, I gave an unscripted speech in Halifax last year and a reporter wrote a newspaper article the next day in which he quoted me. I upbraided my staff and said, "I did not say that. I want an apology and a printed retraction from that reporter." My executive assistant came back a couple of days later, handed me a written transcript and pointed out, "That *was* what you said; we took it off the tape." The reporter had quoted me precisely. "Well," I defended myself, "I may have said that but I didn't mean it "that" way and he didn't put the right inflection on my words. Nonetheless, send the reporter an apology." And my EA said, "You don't have to because I never told him you were quibbling with him"; which explains why I have an EA.

So, if you'll bear with me, my remarks are not scripted but are based on my nearly six years' experience in this headquarters. In that time, I have participated in the preparation and dénouement of the 1987 White Paper, in the budgets of 1989 and 1990, and in this defence policy. I propose to address your topic under a number of headings.

You will recall that some of the things we talked about last year were the appropriate numbers we should have in the armed forces, the question of East confronting West in Europe, our financial situation and, of course, the domestic issues. We conceded we probably had not given those last issues the attention they deserved because of our concentration on war-fighting capabilities.

Let's begin with the number of people in the armed forces. You now know what we have proposed and we can discuss that during the course of the morning. In terms of East versus West, the breakup of the Warsaw Pact and the pace of change in that area, including the demise of the Cold War, far exceeded anybody's expectations. With regard to the financial situation, it is worse now than it was last year; and with regard to domestic issues, the need to remain sensitive to them has not changed at all. Indeed, because of the expectations of our population, that need has increased in the minds of some.

One thing beyond resolution when we met last year was the Gulf War which had just begun. We all know how that worked out — satisfactorily for some and very unsatisfactorily for the thousands of people who died, mostly on the Iraqi side. And unsatisfactorily also in the minds of others because the situation was not fully resolved — although I believe the coalition's decision to cease hostilities when we did was quite right.

One benefit of our participation in that war, and also in the unfortunate operation that took place here in Canada shortly before the Gulf War, was that the public had a chance to see their armed forces in a way that they had not before. I think they were very generally pleased and proud. We engendered a great deal of goodwill towards the armed forces, interest in our ability to take on the tasks that we were given, and debate on whether we had the fiscal and the public support necessary. All that has been useful to us. I think it helped us and I think it helped Minister Masse in getting the new defence policy approved in September.

But admiration and confidence are fickle; they are transitory. We cannot live off our past. We have to continue to demonstrate our utility and our necessity to a public that faces many other problems, mainly economic. The public will have to be convinced of our relevance.

The policy which Mr. Masse announced in September addressed each of the issues I have just mentioned: affordability and balance in forces, East-West détente, and our willingness to continue to address domestic issues. The degree to which we can do that in the new policy, and the degree to which the public will continue to support us in the funding of a policy planned over a 15-year period, remains to be seen.

To my way of thinking, and I believe I reflect the views of many of you, the principal benefit of, and the keystone argument in the defence policy, which the government accepted and promulgated, was the fact that our armed forces need to have a basic war-fighting capability in each of the sea, land and air components. If that is stating the obvious, this audience knows there are many who feel there is no longer a need to have troops that can fight. They feel that Canada, surrounded by three oceans and one very benevolent superpower to our south, should put its capabilities, at least on the military side, towards humanitarian use and peacekeeping.

Bernard Wood is quite right in saying we don't have to consider doing everything from a military perspective and that we have to be more selective in our roles. But that doesn't mean we should not be able to fight; indeed, if we are to have armed forces, I would stipulate that the only reason for having them is that they can do that. That they can perform the other roles is fine, but unless they can fight, this country is spending money needlessly. Other people could carry out those non-fighting tasks for much less money.

But in this speech, I will confine myself to touching on a couple of specific points that deal with your topic: *"Leaner and Meaner — the Armed Forces in the Post-Gulf Era."*

It is difficult for me to translate into French the expression "leaner and meaner." I don't know whether it comes out as "less fat and more efficient" or "slim and ugly." So first let me speak to the title you have selected. Then, I will address the role Canada is called upon to play as a member of our alliances and examine the costs involved. And finally, I will look at infrastructure: equipment, the Total Force concept, and the armed forces structure.

In Calgary the other night I noted that you could make the argument that we don't need any defence at all. We have a small community in Canada that is interested in defence. We have a vocal few who would make an argument that we don't need armed forces in a country our size and with our geography.

One small portion — though large in the minds of some — of our national budget is spent on defence: eight percent of government spending to be exact. We spend five times as much on social services and I think we would agree that's as it should be. This year, we are spending nearly one and a half times as much on unemployment insurance as on defence. The budget for unemployment insurance is approximately $17.2 billion and rising. We spend three times more servicing the public debt — $41 billion this year — than we do on defence. And there are those who would ask: "Alright, for $12 billion, do we really get something that is useful and could we not better use the money somewhere else?"

We could cut the last cent from defence and still have an annual deficit of somewhere between $18 and $20 billion. I used that argument on Michael Wilson a couple of years ago in front of the ERC but it didn't get me anywhere. But if we stopped all spending on defence we would immediately add 117,000 people, military and civilian, to the unemployment roles. We would leave parts of the country without any federal spending and perhaps without any source of income. We would make it painful for industries large and small that depend either on defence contracts or on defence installations in their location. We would also leave to others the defence of our country with all that that means for our sovereignty.

I think there are few people in this country who really mean that we should not have defence of some sort. For the rest, it's proper that debate continue on the nature of our defence. Perhaps we have not got it right yet. So from that point of view, I think your topic is well chosen.

I know what the intent of "leaner and meaner" is: we are going to be smaller and for that obvious reason we are going to be leaner. I could be facetious and say we are going to be meaner because we are going to be smaller and we don't like it, or because we didn't get a pay raise this year, and there might be some truth in that. But what I think you are suggesting is that by becoming smaller we can be more effective. If that's the case, I'm not sure you are right. If the implication is that as we get smaller we must put more money into the results we get out of defence, particularly at the shooting end, the pointy end, then that is a reasonable proposition. But there are aspects of it that bear discussion.

I have made the point on occasion to Cabinet, and it's been accepted, I think, that less means less. If you, the Government, give us less money for defence, you'll get less of a defence product. You can have it any way you like: put money into personnel, put money into infrastructure, or put money into something that makes a bang and does something for you in terms of your Canadian foreign policy. You have to understand that when we get less money it means we are going to stop doing some things we did before. It doesn't mean we won't try and do some things better, but it means some of the things that we have taken for granted as being necessary in the past, and that this country has expected us to do in the past, will not get done. So from that point of view, leaner is right.

In fact, as the new defence policy shows, we have embarked on reductions. This is in keeping with the realities of the world, that is, the change in East-West relations versus the instability that still exists and for which we must be prepared, and the need to tighten our belts and expect less because of the dire financial straits in this country.

It was on that basis that our defence policy foresaw a zero percent real growth into the next century. We have had to modify it for a number of reasons, and I will talk about those in a moment, under the headings of infrastructure and personnel. Nonetheless, by accepting that less means less, we have decided to do away almost completely with our forces stationed in Europe. We'll reduce the core mechanized brigade group to nil strength by 1994, the air division the same way, and repatriate the people and the equipment. This will leave only a task force of 1,100 troops in Europe, plus the forces of the AWACS airborne early warning system in Geilenkirchen.

We have foresworn doing some of the things we thought were vital but could no longer do. The CH-147 has been taken out of operation and we have thus lost our heavy helicopter lift. We accepted some time ago that we could not purchase nuclear submarines and therefore we have foresworn the capability of going under the ice into our third ocean. We have accepted that as we come out of Europe, our ability to maintain a capability in the main battle-tank area is finished. However, we will not do away with the direct fire support armoured capability.

We have also accepted that less means cutting headquarters and overhead, but also in the operational area too. We had already begun to do so by taking out the tracker aircraft earlier and thus losing the medium-range patrol aircraft function. As we get squeezed further in the future, we'll have to make the same kind of decisions and adjust some of the things we have taken for granted in the past. As Mr. Wood has said, in this much more specialized world, our ability to be all things to all people is not within the range of our pocketbook. In terms of meaner — more bang for the buck — he's right.

It's easy to talk about slogans. It's easy to let roll off the tongue things like "leaner and meaner" and "flexible and more mobile." Sometimes, putting them into effect and really understanding what we mean by them is more difficult.

We have long accepted that we probably have too many headquarters and they are too large. We are moving to reduce a number of them. Some as a result of our 1989 budget and the cutting of bases and stations; some by the re-organization of the land force into geographic areas combining both regulars and reserves under one single command, and a reduction in the number of district headquarters; in other areas by reducing the size of national defence headquarters by a thousand, with an approximate even split between military and civilians. But there comes a point beyond which you cannot reduce your overhead no matter how lean you want to be, and no matter how mean you want to be. Certain things have to get done and you need people in the right place to do them.

So we are reducing our force in terms of percentages to try and keep the same level of command structure and the same ratio of NCMs to officers and officers to general officers. Over the next two years, general officers will be reduced by twenty percent and colonels by fifteen percent. That is a start.

Some people have used the fact we have a lot of generals in the forces to criticize the armed forces or to poke fun at it. A number of you have had fun writing letters to editors saying the armed forces have too many generals and no troops. We do have a lot of generals: 116 in the Regular Force right now. Part of that reflects the price of belonging to alliances and I'm going to talk about alliances in a moment.

We made a decision in this country around 1917 that we would never again allow Canadian troops to be put into battle without Canadians being in a position to influence how they were used. We joined NATO, we joined NORAD, and when we committed troops to the United Nations, we determined we would have our share in making those decisions.

For that reason, we have 12 officers with NATO — general officers. We have some 5 or 6 with NORAD and 3 with the United Nations. Is that too many for a force of 86,000 regular? Of course it is! Does it mean they are not doing useful work? Of course it does not!

We have 8 specialist generals if you include our doctors, our lawyer, our dentists and our padres. Do they have to be generals? Probably not. In terms of their specialty, they can do what they do very well without wearing a rank, but it has been our tradition — that's why we call them Surgeon Generals, Judge Advocate General, Chaplains General — and our means of recognizing professionalism in areas unrewarded by financial remuneration. But, could we get away with having lesser ranks there? Sure we could.

We will cut generals, but not for the reason the public, the press and indeed some of you ladies and gentlemen seem to think we should. We are doing it as much for perception as anything else, to demonstrate to the troops that they are not the only ones taking cuts. In some cases, senior civilians will take over the roles of some generals because the equipment procurement and handling some of the very large programs will still have to be done by service people.

So leaner and meaner is fine but there comes a point beyond which you cannot cut what you call the fat or the tail, not if we are going to make the whole operation of our forces effective. Let me go on now to the next topic which is alliances.

I mentioned that Canada long ago decided our defence role is more efficiently fulfilled as a member of alliances than as a single country. It is obvious that with our vast country and small population, we cannot defend such a large territory or independently influence world affairs on our own. In a sense, Canada has little choice but to assume a significant role as one of the richest countries in the world (amongst the 7 richest) despite a small population and armed forces. Many countries, including our allies, rely on us to participate in a variety of fields be they political, diplomatic, financial or humanitarian. They also expect the help of our armed forces when that is necessary.

For very sound reasons, therefore, we decided to become a member of alliances. Even though East-West confrontations have ended, our involvement in alliance security has not. On the contrary, as things stand, NATO is perceived as the only pillar of stability in the world today. It was recognized as such by the old Warsaw Pact even prior to the collapse of the Cold War. I am certain there are now many countries from Eastern Europe, including Russia and members of the Commonwealth of Independent States, who wish to join NATO. NATO will continue to exist in all sorts of forms, including a military form, and Canada will continue to be a member of NATO.

This choice is not without cost. Our decision means that certain elements of the armed forces will be left in Europe on a full-time basis: our commitment to the AMF(L) in Norway will endure; one of our ships will remain with the Standing Naval Force Atlantic to continue playing a role in the North Atlantic and we have dedicated one contingency brigade and two tactical squadrons for deployment anywhere in the world, including Europe under NATO command.

In North America, NORAD will also prevail to the end of the century, albeit with changes. As things stand, Canada and the United States are committed to this alliance. In the aftermath of the break-up of the Soviet Union, it is unclear who holds the reins of power there and the possibility of threat to North America cannot be discounted. Just recently, the *Globe and Mail* published an article stating that within eight years about twenty countries will possess ballistic missiles. More than half a dozen of these countries will have a strike range extending as far as five thousand kilometres.

All this to say that North American airspace may be free of threats from Soviet or Russian bombers but not from missiles. NORAD is still very much a valid requirement and, having signed a five-year extension to the agreement, Canada remains a partner. Undoubtedly, we will have to adjust our perception of what NORAD should be, as well as Canada's role within the alliance. Perhaps we'll focus on space programs rather than on air defence. This is something we will have to examine over the next five years.

Beyond the North American Air Defence Agreement, our other military arrangements with the United States, under the CANUS agreements, will continue. The threats to the North American land mass are minor compared to other concerns elsewhere. Nonetheless, the first role of any armed force is to defend its country. If we don't play our role in the defence of North America, others will do it for us at a price. And you know what that price is.

My final point on alliances is to note the experience of the Gulf War and the coalition. The ability of countries from many disparate backgrounds to operate together demonstrated the value of alliances. Here I'm talking about the NATO or ABCA countries which have either alliances or agreements, and which exchange operational procedures (STAMAGs). The fact that we have trained together for so long in Europe, particularly on the air and naval side, demonstrated its efficacy when we went to war together. The value of belonging to alliances, if only for that reason, is clear.

Let's talk about infrastructure for a moment. It's a discussion that doesn't stop. It is a very emotive point and understandably so. You know the simplistic equation of personnel costs, O & M costs and capital costs, the last one normally being the residual, and I will talk about equipment in a moment. There is no question that to be meaner as we become leaner, we have to reduce our infrastructure. Not because we want to or because having infrastructure in certain places doesn't serve a useful purpose, but from the purely military perspective. If we want to get bang for our buck and demonstrate to Canadians that they are getting value for money, we have to examine our infrastructure.

That decision was deferred under the defence policy. Indeed, the deferral was the reason we were able to get the defence policy approved. The panel appointed by Mr. Masse will make recommendations to government on the question of infrastructure in the Canadian Forces. We spend a lot of money we can ill afford on O & M. It costs us personnel because if we retain unaffordable infrastructure, the personnel costs remain alongside the O & M costs. We have to review the maintenance of infrastructure which has grown old, just as so many of our cities, towns and villages must do.

If we don't address O & M costs, what will result, at the other end of the scale in a fixed budget, is a loss of operational effectiveness. It is a valid debating point that the Defence Department does more for national values by spending money in deprived areas of the country than by providing bang for buck. If regional employment is seen as an essential task for DND, we should continue doing it, but it will be at the expense of value for money in defence capability. We will have to wait and see. The panel has not made its recommendations yet.

My only point would be that it is incumbent on us to demonstrate to the political decision-makers how wisely we spend money on defence. We have to make it abundantly clear that, in an era of diminishing revenue, spending money for reasons that are not purely defensive has a cost, and the cost is operational effectiveness. I and my advisors will be criticized for not carrying out military roles unless there is an understanding by all Canadians of what the infrastructure equation means. In that scenario (providing employment rather than defence) there will be those who will be disappointed or who will say we are not getting value for money. Their criticism will be based on our inability to advise government on the efficacy of the equipment needed by the armed forces to meet operational roles. That has not happened yet but it could happen in the future.

In terms of equipment, we both know the areas in which we are deficient. At our low point in the late 1960s, early '70s, we spent less than 7 percent of our defence budget on capital equipment and we are living with the results of that decision today. We have been down to 18 percent, we have got it up to 22 percent right now, our target is 26 percent over the next five years and finally 30 percent. This is about the maximum that most of our NATO allies are spending on their equipment.

Some say striving for the target at the expense of personnel is misplaced. They say that we should insist on matching the right number of people to the equipment we can afford in due course, and worry less about putting money into a capital budget that needs to be moved from 22 percent to 30 percent. And that too is an argument. I think it's a false argument, because we cannot train the people to the appropriate levels; we cannot meet the contingencies which, although not as urgent in reaction time as they were at the height of East/West confrontation, nonetheless, still require us to be ready to go at fairly short notice to do tasks demanding modern equipment. The Gulf war is a case in point. We were able to bring our ships up to an adequate state of armament simply because the equipment was available for our new vessels. We must not put ourselves in the position where we have a lot of dedicated troops losing interest because they have nothing to train with.

That noted, it may be that the way we procured equipment in the past has been more luxurious than we can afford. We tend to go, for all the right reasons, for the best equipment able to do the job. We set standards in our requests for proposal that we consider to be absolutely essential for doing our jobs. Then we spend a lot of money making sure one hundred percent effectiveness is achieved. It may be that we could spend a lot less money by getting equipment that is ninety percent effective. Maybe the time, effort and man-hours spent on getting that other ten percent is misplaced. That is something we are asking

ADM(Mat) and the DCDS to look at as they work the programs through the PCB and into the capital account.

Perhaps, because we wish to maintain our own industries in this country, and because we wish to put money from the defence budget back into the local economy, we will continue to pay a premium for what we produce in Canada or for the cost-shared benefits of the equipment we buy abroad. That is part and parcel of doing business, but there are probably areas where we can buy, with less certainty of absolute perfection, while meeting most of our requirements and getting more equipment. That is something all of us have to look at and accept. All that noted, we must be certain the equipment that we do get meets Total Force requirements.

Let me talk about Total Force because, like "leaner and meaner" "highly mobile" and "flexible", it may mean something or it may mean nothing. You represent associations that in many cases are largely Reserve-oriented. You know the difficulties that have existed over the past half century between Reserve and Regular forces: the suspicions, the rivalries and the outright feeling of abandonment that has occurred from time to time. Your concerns are right and your concerns need to be addressed.

But the general population of this country doesn't really care whether it's a Reserve or a Regular soldier that does the job. They just want it done in the most efficient way with the least money. They should expect that.

Up until 1939 that defence product was best produced by a relatively large Reserve and by a very small Regular cadre which existed only to prepare the Reserves for operations. We reverted to that role at the end of World War II for about five years because that again met expectations. But a lot changed after 1950. We agreed to be a sovereign nation involved in the solution of world problems far beyond anything we had done before. At that time, as you recall, the Reserves were reduced both in numbers and in efficacy, and the Regular force was increased to meet the requirements of the Korean War and later the requirements of the Cold War.

Maybe Canada could meet its present defence needs most effectively by having a force that is almost entirely Regular and no Reserves (or very few Reserves and those only in specialized areas). Certainly the requirement for speedy reaction to a monolithic East European and Soviet force has disappeared and therefore the reaction time to produce forces is much less than it used to be.

Nonetheless, Canada has taken on international operational roles for its armed forces, as well as for its diplomatic functions, that demand a capability to put troops at very short notice, full time, into a number of different areas. Our current thirteen peacekeeping operations demand troops abroad continuously. Other commitments I have mentioned have ships at sea, aircraft in the air and troops committed to go to Norway. These require full-time forces.

So why spend money on the Reserves if our tasks can be done efficiently in this day and age? We don't expect mobilization? So we don't expect to fight the kind of war we mobilized our Reserves for three times in this century?

You could take the opposite position and say that Canada's role internationally need no longer be a purely defensive one — only in times of crisis. Since we are pulling most of our troops out of Europe and since the capability for contingency operations can be met by small cadres of Regulars and large Reserve groups, we can reduce the Regular force to a very small size and have a very large Reserve with most of the defence money going into equipping, training, and manning the Reserve slots. You know I'm going to say that the answer lies somewhere in between and, of course, it does.

The requirements of the armed forces differ in the navy, in the army, in the air force, in the communications, in the logistics, in the engineering, and in the medical worlds. Our ability to meet national requirements varies as we talk about each of those capabilities. Our need for Reserve elements may be far more necessary in one area than in another.

What is certain is that in today's budgetary situation, meeting our obligations — the ones that this country has expected us to carry out and, indeed, has demanded us to carry out, and for which they pay us twelve billion dollars a year — can only be done by a much closer integration of Reserve and Regular units, part-time and full-time troops. And if we don't make that mix work, then we will not be meeting the country's expectations.

As I mentioned, this depends greatly on which organization is targeted. The navy's case obviously differs from that of the air force or the army. As a matter of a fact, the navy has been relatively unaffected by the defence policy announced in September. The Regular force strength will remain the same whereas the naval Reserve ranks will increase. As you can see, less actually means less, but in the navy's case more means more. Here I'm talking about the Maritime Coastal Defence Vessels. These ships will be equipped and manned by the Reserves for their new role.

Now for the air force. If I were to ask General Huddleston, he would probably tell me he would not have enough people to meet his role were it not for the Reserves' contribution: aircraft, pilots or crews. For example, we have a Reserve squadron in full-time support of the navigation school in Winnipeg. On each air force base which supports aircraft, the support role is possible only because of the dedicated efforts of air force reservist technicians who give a day or two each week to help out their Regular force counterparts.

It is apparent that where the amalgamation of Reserve and Regular force already works, we should reinforce success. There are however cases were this blend is not so easily achieved. In the army, bringing together a formation that can work as a formation is no easy task, especially when the smallest formation is a brigade. A great many factors such as equipment, organization, time, training areas and the nature of the Reservist all make this a challenging undertaking. Furthermore, most Reservists are students who have a great deal of time at their disposal during the summer, but not so much during the rest of the year. Also, most of them leave the Reserves upon graduation.

So General Gervais and his Reserve generals in the army have a much harder task in putting together the kind of force that will meet the army's immediate requirements.

In terms of Total Force: on the Regular side, regiments, units and organizations are being examined, and if necessary amalgamated or cut. The same thing will have to happen with our Reserves. If we have the right balance of units, good; if we don't, we must change them. Either we re-role them, or disband them, or amalgamate them. And those are tough changes to consider given our history. But our history is 20/20; our future is not clear. If we are going to produce forces that meet the requirements of the country, that can demonstrate to the public that doesn't know Reserve from Regular, or part-time from full-time, and doesn't care (that's not quite true because in certain areas where regiments or units bear the name of towns and provinces, there is a great deal of caring) then the bottom line has to be efficient armed forces.

If we have to make some changes that are tough and that violate our ideas of history, so be it. Total Force will only mean what we want it to. We in the NDHQ are trying to get away from the idea of just talking about Total Force. We are demanding that it become a reality. If Total Force is to be effective, we all have to look upon it that way.

I wanted to conclude by talking about force structure and in a sense, I have already done that. So, I would like to summarize it. Our navy is going to maintain a blue water capability. That is what we mean by having combat capable armed forces in the navy. Sixteen destroyers and frigates into the middle of the next decade and three of an eventual six submarines based on today's anticipated budget. Twelve maritime coastal defence vessels, four of an eventual six corvettes and the bits and pieces that go along to make that kind of a navy effective. On the air side, new ship borne helicopters and long-range patrol aircraft.

Our army will be based on three operational brigade groups, largely Regular but with considerable Reserve input, and a number of training brigades under the command of each of the four areas, the last two of which will be stood up this summer. We will maintain the commitment to the Ace Mobile Force from inside the three brigades; we will maintain an 1,100-man battle group (half-armoured, half-infantry, support battery, reconnaissance troop, engineer troop) in Europe in a place and role to be defined. At the moment we think that role will probably be in a multinational corps, perhaps in a multinational reconnaissance brigade of that corps, lodging on a base at a cost of about $157 million a year. That allows us to save the $1.25 billion we have been spending on CFE per year. We will have a contingency brigade group in this country ready to be sent anywhere in the world for any kind of operational task supported by sea and air. The brigade group will not necessarily be a specific one from the three brigade groups in the country. It will probably be based on one of them and tailored with the right kind of units needed for the right kind of tasks when the time comes. We will have the ability to make it sustainable by using those other two brigade groups to form replacements and by calling up and putting together other replacement brigade groups from the training brigades that the areas will put together themselves. Again, these will be largely Reserve but with some Regular in them.

On the air force side, there is a continued commitment to both the navy and the army in areas that are specific to them — tactical helicopters for the army, long-range patrol and anti-submarine aircraft with their own fighting capability in the case of the navy. As well, there will be four fighter squadrons: two assigned to NORAD, two for worldwide contingency roles, another fighter squadron for training purposes, and of course our continuing requirements in search and rescue and long-range transport. The latter is an area in which we have been doing such sterling work in the past year in terms of humanitarian assistance around the world and now into the former Soviet Union.

As I said before, the requirements are different for sea, land and air, but the one basic requirement we have insisted on, and the government has agreed to, is that there should be fighting capabilities in each of those. We have tried to balance the resources as best we can, given our anticipated requirements, into those three different areas.

My final point has to do with national unity, a subject which is on all of our minds. The greatest problem we face in this country is not a threat from without but a threat from within. Whatever our feelings, my opinion is that our best future lies in remaining as one nation and not as two or three or four.

I raise the point here because you are aware of the discussions that have taken place regarding the possible use of the armed forces following decisions that come out of the constitutional debate. You will be aware also that I felt an obligation to enter that debate simply because we were having too many questions asked by the troops. The field was being left too uneven in favour of the academics, the lawyers and the politicians who would like to use it for their own specific purposes. I'm not arguing their right to do that. In fact, it needed to be done.

Nonetheless, we have made the point that the armed forces are not part of that equation. We all have interests in the outcome but if we don't have the common sense, the compassion, the sense of compromise and understanding necessary to keep this country together by peaceful means, then we certainly don't have the right to fight to keep it together, nor shall we.

On the other hand, we do have an agency for stability in this country in the armed forces, both Regular and Reserve. We represent a quintessentially national community of people from all parts of the country, from both linguistic groups, who serve well together anywhere in the world. They understand the fortune that we have in this country, particularly when juxtaposed to countries that are less fortunate.

By demonstrating to the Canadian public that we are an agency for stability, we can keep the debate on an even basis and free of civil-war rhetoric. In doing so we will be carrying out our most important responsibility.

Thank you very much ladies and gentlemen.

Questions & Answers

Q. Major General Lionel Bourgeois, Air Force Association

We in the Air Force Associations are fully committed to the Total Force Air Force, as you would put it in your terms, one Air Force, regular and reserve. We can't look at that without looking at our 'cradle', where our young airmen come from. The Royal Canadian Air Cadets, over the last fifty years, having trained almost one million young men and women, is part of that for us. Your department spends some sixty million dollars per year for all three groups of cadets in Canada, and one could perhaps equate that to about one thousand dollars per cadet for summer camps, training, uniforms, etc. In times of decreasing dollars, there is a great temptation to take a look at that, not only centrally, but also by Base Commanders and Unit Commanders, to trim the support they have given in the past. What do you see as the future for our cradle?

A. That's a very topical question. My short answer is that we're not going to decrease funding to cadets at all, in fact, in some areas we might be increasing it. You understand that the cadet organizations are not part of the Canadian Forces. The cadet instructor list is, and the number of people we assign from the regular force, and the Air Force Associations and the reserves assign, to look after cadets is large, and so it should be. Next to the Boy Scouts of Canada, of which I am the National Vice President, it is the best youth organization in the country. (You wouldn't expect me not to say that — and we don't compete with each other, scouts normally ends by the age of 14!) We are very much aware of the degree to which the men and women who come into the armed forces, either as officers or as NCMs, have a background in cadets. Our difficulty at the moment is that we can't take as many of them into the armed forces as we would like because, as you know, part of our downsizing programme we are having to shut recruiting down considerably. In fact, we are only going to take 2,000 recruits in next year, as opposed to the 3,200 we took in this year, and the 7,000 we took the year before. From that point of view, we are not able to take as many as we have given education and training to in the cadet corps, and as would like to join the Canadian Forces. But let me assure you that it is not our intention to cut the support that we give to the cadets, in fact, quite the contrary. We do recognize that not only do cadet programmes provide good training for our youth, they are also a good way of keeping the public in touch with what we in the armed forces are trying to achieve.

I would like to build on this question, and make a remark about an article that appeared in the *Ottawa Sun* a short time ago. The journalist was commenting on the fact that an individual had come to us for funding for a study which would examine whether there should be some form of conscription in Canada to account for the fact that a number of young men and women are leaving school without a job, or without adequate training, and what better way to bring them into the work force than to put them into the armed forces, give them a skill and some employment in those formative years and then send them on their way. The journalist's point was that we had denied funding, that the generals weren't interested and maybe the generals should be. I can invite you to imagine what the headline might have been had the generals said "yes, let's have conscription, and we'll fund it." All that said, there is a lot to be said for using armed forces in a time of financial crisis, to assist both people who are out of work and to develop youth. We have had a number of programmes over the last 30 years, the Student Youth Employment Programme and others, that have done just that. We would be open to doing something like that, but of course, these things cost money and less means less. So if we do that we may be doing something else less, unless we got incremental funding. I make this point just to demonstrate that we are not turning our backs simply for fiscal reasons on the youth which is our future and, indeed, a very important part of this country.

Q. Brigadier General (Retired) Michael Weber

In a rather passing remark, you referred to abandoning the plan to acquire a nuclear submarine capability and, therefore, automatically abandoning the role of sovereignty in the Arctic. This seemed to rather lightly taken, except for a few editorials. My question is, was there any serious discussion over this being a great lack in our national strategy? Is there any sense today, among our political masters, that there is a gap in our defence arrangement, when we apparently have no feeling of responsibility for the Arctic?

A. That's a topical question which was raised yesterday by the CDA Policy Committee in a meeting with Minister Masse, myself and other senior officials from the department, although it was posed not purely from the point of view of nuclear submarines. You could argue, and I certainly would, that sovereignty in our Arctic does not depend solely on nuclear submarines. We do have means of exercising sovereignty, however imperfectly, without going under the ice. But you are quite right, we have abandoned what we consider our ocean to others. Less means less, and where can we use our money more effectively. We demonstrate our sovereignty in the Arctic region, partly by the fact that we have one station there, which no one knows too much about, but which is there. We will further enhance our capability of demonstrating sovereignty by sensor systems under the ice. We do have aerial patrols that cover our northern region on a routine basis, probably not as much as we would like, (less means less), but we did buy the Arturas aircraft in addition to the Aurora just so we could expand our reach. There has been talk, on a number of occasions, that we should put more troops in the north. As I asked your Defence Policy Committee, tell me to do what, and where, and we'll consider it. It is simple to say, "let's open up a base and we'll do some northern training." We have to understand what we mean by 'northern training'. Does it mean that we going to run around the tundra? No, the Federal Environment Review Agency won't allow us to do that. To counter what threat? Is it just to demonstrate that we are there, and it is Canadian? We can do that with a member of the RCMP and a flag. We have a programme to increase the number of Forward Operating Localities for our fighters in the north, as part of our NORAD agreement. In many cases, we are doing that over the objections of the locals, who don't want us in their area. So, it is difficult for us to determine what would be a cost-effective and useful deployment of our resources in the north, if it is simply to demonstrate that we are interested in our sovereignty. You will recall that the ice-breaker was to be built just to demonstrate that purpose and we were to spend a lot of money in building it. That too went the way of the budget. Getting back to your question, has the government abrogated its responsibility in this area? I don't think so. I think it is a good political football for opposition parties, whose job it is to oppose. Put into power themselves, would they come up with any other solution? I don't know. At the moment, given the resources we have, and given the task we have, we feel they are better applied in the way we are proceeding. But we are not ignoring the Arctic. We do train there; we do support the idea of Ranger groups that develop a presence, in fact, we are increasing the number of Rangers. But the concept of spending large amounts of money to put people in an area where we can't train, and where environmentalists worry about what we're doing, is not attractive. We haven't, however, abandoned the north.

Q. Colonel Murray Johnston, CDA Vice Chairman, Ontario

In reference to your comments on infrastructure, you spoke about the matter of making savings because costs were not related directly to defence, but perhaps to subsidizing, or keeping remote areas going. My question is, are you able to identify those two costs, the defence costs and subsidization cost? And is it worthwhile to do it? Secondly, I have a related question dealing with the military collections and museums that are on bases. Would you comment on the consideration of their disposition in your infrastructure studies?

A. It is very hard, as you know, to get a grip on the costs of a base, and it's particularly hard for a base commander whose ability to influence those costs is very minimal. That is why we have put together this study that examines the degree to which we can give a base commander autonomy over spending decisions. We can certainly make a judgement on our ability to afford the number of organizations of a certain type. Can we, in a force this size, afford as many bases as we have? Can we afford this many training institutions, or can we amalgamate these institutions environmentally? Do we need as many supply depots? Military colleges? The list goes on. In certain areas we can demonstrate that costs can be saved, but are there political considerations, in a country of dual nature like this one, that would mitigate against us making some economies. The answer may be yes, and if that's the price of unity, so be it. All that to say, in terms of getting bang for buck, if you're spending a lot of money on tail and less on teeth, it may be because you are doing things that you don't absolutely have to do. What we are trying to do is identify what those are, and then answer the political imperatives of whether we should, or should not, get rid of them.

To a degree, that applies to the question of military museums, although there is more a sense of ethos, heart and tradition which, in spite of what you may think, we are not losing sight of, in terms of what we're trying to achieve with a reduced budget and with reduced forces. In fact, tradition and esprit is the basis of all of what we do. Although I must tell you that we are trying to come to grips with the question of military ethos, and what that means in the latter part of this century, in a time when social values and social changes are occurring and modifying so quickly. We are examining museums. Our Minister has a very great interest in museums, having been Minister of Communications, and being an intellectual very much interested in our national heritage, he has more than a passing interest in how we're handling museums.

Q. Major Eileen Butson, Defence Medical Association

You have said that, if we have to make changes that violate our ideas of history, then so be it. I think it is very important to defend our institutions, because that is our country. Our

institutions are very important to many of us. It causes disunity
if we feel our traditions and institutions are being forgotten.

A. I agree with you. You've just heard me say that ethos, tradition
and esprit are very close to us. Indeed, it's what makes soldiers,
sailors, airmen and airwomen fight. We have to awfully careful
how we demonstrate that to those with sharp pencils in Finance
and Treasury Board and, indeed, in Cabinet. We have to be
very careful that we are not putting money into things simply
for their own sake, or for the sake that you and I and others
here, understand the value of them, whereas others don't. We
are growing increasingly past that point where Canadians have
an understanding of Canadian military heritage. Most of what
they see on the airwaves is not Canadian. They did become
more aware of the imperatives of war as a result of the Gulf
War. But to many, those things that *we know* are the requirements to get people to fight, may not be so clear to them.

We will protect institutions. Those that we cannot justify,
for a variety of reasons, may have to be looked at very carefully.

III

Police and Military Cooperation in Canada

by
Assistant Commissioner Mike Thivierge
Royal Canadian Mounted Police

It is a pleasure for me to speak to you today on the relationship between the military and the police, specifically the RCMP. This relationship, of course, is not a new one. As some of you may already know, the history of RCMP/military relations actually dates back to 1885 when RCMP members performed military service during the North West Rebellion. RCMP officers afterwards went on to serve in the Boer War, the First World War, the Russian Civil War and the Second World War. Of course, both the extent and the nature of cooperation between the Canadian military and the RCMP has greatly changed since, particularly when we consider the multitude of changes that have occurred in the post-World War Two era.

Canada's population growth, changes in our social, political and economic environment, as well as the development of advanced technology, have not only changed the fabric of Canadian life, but also increased and altered the challenges faced by law enforcement. With new problems must come new approaches and solutions. Today it is no longer possible to live or work in isolation. The world we live in has truly become a global village. Often, events that occur thousands of miles away impact on us directly. This is also true for the law enforcement community.

Our task becomes even more challenging when we consider that the availability of resources seems to be forever shrinking. As a consequence, there has never been a greater need to work together. If there is a theme that I would like to underscore, it is partnership.

Today, police cooperation with the Canadian military is but one example of such an approach. Over the past two decades, we have benefitted in many ways from the assistance of the military. Such cooperation is helping promote effective responses to many law enforcement challenges.

Size and Diversity of Canada

Bearing in mind my brief, introductory remarks, let us now dwell on the country we police. Policing this country is no small task. Canada, in terms of land mass, is the largest country in the world and is populated by over 26 million people. As you know, its territory ranges from wide fertile prairies and farmlands, to great areas of mountains, rocks and lakes, to northern wilderness and arctic tundra. Canada's coastlines are among the longest in the world. The total area of Canada is close to 10 million square kilometres. Our boundary with the United States, which covers about 9,000 kilometres, is the longest unprotected border in the world.

We have over 2,000 airports, some 2,000 undocumented airstrips and 42 principal ports. Some 16 million registered vehicles tread over about 280,000 kilometres of federal/provincial roads and highways. As anyone can see, the enormity and diversity of the country make policing Canada a most ambitious task. The police have their hands full, and assistance from outside agencies, such as DND, is not only helpful but, I maintain, essential.

Memorandums of Understanding

RCMP enforcement capabilities are enhanced through cooperation and assistance from various government departments, including the Department of National Defence. This assistance comes largely in the form of intelligence exchange, planning, and communications and logistical support. In most cases, the relationship is managed through memorandums of understanding.

These agreements cover a wide range of areas, from assistance and service to RCMP members in United Nations Peacekeeping operations, to cooperation in research and development. One area of research, for example, relates to the disposal of explosives equipment. The basic philosophy behind these agreements is to avoid duplication and to better manage resources. For example, we are not in the air force or navy business; but, if we require the use of sophisticated aircraft or ships, why not rely on the people who are in that business? I will now focus, for the most part, on areas where we have ongoing cooperation with DND.

Drug Enforcement

Canadian military support of RCMP drug enforcement efforts has brought considerable success. While combating the illicit drug problem from the demand reduction perspective requires educational efforts, combating the problem from the supply side, of course, involves interdiction. This assistance for the most part covers aid in interdiction efforts. When requested, DND aids in the surveillance and detection of vessels, aircraft and vehicles suspected of smuggling illegal drugs. It also provides suitable platforms to transport RCMP apprehension teams to interdiction sites.

The RCMP first approached DND for drug interdiction assistance in the late 1970's. By that time, the use of motherships to import large quantities of illegal drugs began to increase. To make things worse, this trend was occurring while the RCMP was disbanding what remained of its marine division. The RCMP's offshore enforcement capability was rapidly reduced and, in 1978, the Force approached the military for vessel support for a West Coast importation attempt. Two destroyers assisted in this venture and 27 tons of marijuana were interdicted.

The operation's success led to an informal agreement, whereby DND would provide assistance to us on an ad hoc basis. By 1987, however, a memorandum of understanding was established which defined the terms and procedures for provision of assistance.

By the terms of this agreement, intelligence sharing and liaison were established to exchange strategic profiles of suspect vessels and their movements. Also, DND assets were made available for maritime operations. Surveillance by aircraft and warship was to be provided for suspect vessels. Surface interdiction operations were to be carried out by warship, and ceilings were established for air hours and ship days. You will note that support at this time was limited to sea operations.

By November 1989, however, with escalating drug smuggling into Canada and the growing wealth and sophistication of drug trafficking organizations, the MOU was reviewed for expansion. For one thing, the offshore limitation was eliminated, meaning that assistance was no longer restricted to territory beyond the 12 mile limit. For another, assistance was expanded to include the support of land and air operations.

This means that, when requested, DND will now provide necessary support for the surveillance and interdiction of suspect aircraft, vehicles and vessels. Likewise, intelligence sharing and liaison have been expanded to include the exchange of strategic profiles of suspect aircraft and vehicles and their movements. Also, under certain guidelines, armed assistance could be provided to RCMP officers.

Besides the review of the 1987 MOU, other measures have also been taken to support RCMP drug enforcement. In December, 1989, a DND liaison officer arrived at the Drug Enforcement Directorate at RCMP Headquarters in Ottawa, to further operational support for RCMP drug enforcement. In July 1991, two more DND persons were added.

Within National Defence Headquarters, a counter-narcotics coordinating committee meets to coordinate initiatives to support the RCMP. Within the Air Force, an aerial counter-narcotics working group pursues air-related initiatives. This group first met in June 1990 and continues to meet on a quarterly basis.

Just as an aside, I would mention here that this is not the first time that DND aerial assets have been used in support of RCMP operations. Such assistance actually dates back to the 1930's, when DND provided aircraft surveillance against rum running operations on the East Coast. In fact, half of the Royal Canadian Air Force civil flying time was allotted to catching prohibition rum runners. Joint RCMP-RCAF surveillance patrols were established and, in 1933, although the RCAF was forbidden to stop and search ships, three landings were made to allow the RCMP to stop smugglers and seize goods. It is interesting to note that, throughout our history, smuggling routes and methods of operation have not changed in a significant way. Today, of course, the smuggled goods are illegal drugs.

With more and more illicit drugs available on the Canadian market, and with police resources limited, assistance from outside agencies has become even more important to the RCMP in its drug enforcement role. In fact, in 1989, an operation which led to the seizure of 500 kilograms of cocaine confirmed that cocaine smuggling into Canada had larger dimensions than previously suspected and that indeed more resources and assistance were needed.

The seizure was made at a small airstrip near Fredericton, New Brunswick, in April 1989. Up until that time, it was the largest cocaine seizure in Canadian history. A twin-engine executive aircraft carrying the drugs had flown non-stop from Colombia. What this operation — known as Operation Overstep — showed us was that Colombian drug cartels had begun to view Canada as a stepping stone to the US market, as well as a potentially lucrative market in its own right. In addition, it highlighted the threat posed by drug smuggling using general aviation aircraft.

From Operation Overstep we learned about the aerial capabilities of the cartels and how they used aircraft to facilitate cocaine traffic between North and South America. We also realized the necessity for increased assistance to combat drug smuggling, especially aerial smuggling. This particular operation gave impetus to the review of the 1987 MOU between the RCMP and DND, which I have already mentioned, to include DND aerial and land assets in addition to the maritime assets already established.

As well, Operation Overstep provided us with yet another example of the violence that accompanies the illicit drug trade. In April of that same year, some six months after the operation was concluded, five South Americans crossed the Canada/US border with an arsenal of weapons and ammunition. They were planning to forcibly free two Colombian pilots who had been apprehended in connection with the seizure. All five were apprehended and arrested.

Since 1987, there have been many successful operations in which the military has directly assisted the RCMP in drug interdiction. A notable example occurred in July 1990 during a sea operation off the east coast of Nova Scotia. The RCMP had requested CP140 Aurora maritime patrol aircraft and a Canadian Armed Forces destroyer to covertly shadow two suspect drug smuggling vessels. This support helped the RCMP to seize over 25 tons of hashish.

NORAD

Additional assistance to RCMP drug interdiction efforts has come about through NORAD. In 1989, NORAD's role was expanded to detect and monitor aerial traffic suspected of carrying illegal drugs into the United States and the periphery of Canada. The counter-narcotics role was formally included as a NORAD mission during the recent May 1991 renewal of the NORAD agreement. Canadian NORAD resources are used to support this mission. These resources include CF18 fighters, air surveillance radars and Canadian service personnel occupying NORAD positions in the United States who have been actively involved in interdiction operations.

In addition to enhancing NORAD's counter-narcotics role, National Defence Headquarters has pursued several initiatives. These initiatives include expanded air support and the implementation of a policy of directed landings, whereby unknown aircraft can be directed to a published port of entry and processed by Canada Customs or the RCMP. NORAD CF18's can be used for these landings. As well, the 180-knot true airspeed threshold has been removed for aircraft operating in the air defence identification zone. Previously, aircraft flying at less than 180 knots would escape the NORAD surveillance network. Now, all aircraft, regardless of speed, must file a flight plan, which of course aids in their tracking, reporting and identification.

Secure communications have been improved and secure Anti-Drug network terminals have been installed in the National Defence Operations Centre, RCMP headquarters and the Canadian NORAD Region. As well, under NORAD policy, Canadian Forces aerial assets and Maritime resources have been involved in a variety of counter-narcotics operations and exercises in support of the RCMP.

Counterterrorism

Another area in which DND assists the RCMP's law enforcement capacity is the area of combating terrorism. Compared to other countries, Canada has been relatively free of terrorist incidents. In the past two decades, however, we too have increasingly experienced alarming acts of politically motivated crime. You will remember, for example, the October crisis of 1970 and the activities of Direct Action in 1982. There have also been terrorist acts by persons using Canada as a stage on which to fight foreign battles. In 1985, terrorists stormed the Turkish embassy in Ottawa, killing a Canadian security guard. The Air India and Narita disasters are further examples.

The RCMP, under the Security Offences Act, is assigned primary peace officer responsibility in relation to criminal offences constituting a threat to the national security of Canada. We also provide protective services for internationally protected persons, foreign missions and international events held in Canada. Our Armed Forces have often assisted us in fulfilling these duties.

For example, DND provided security-related assistance for the Commonwealth Heads of Government Meeting in Vancouver in 1987 and for the Toronto Economic Summit in 1988. Armed assistance was provided for perimeter security during the Vancouver Meeting and for airport security during the Toronto

Summit. We also exchange intelligence regarding threats to internationally protected persons on Canadian Forces Bases.

One of the tools the RCMP has at its disposal to respond to terrorist hostage incidents is our Special Emergency Response Team, known as SERT. SERT may be deployed, with the authorization of the Solicitor General of Canada, in rare cases where efforts to bring about a peaceful conclusion have failed. It is important to keep in mind that members of the SERT are peace officers and therefore remain accountable under the law in conditions where force is used. When force is used, it must always be reasonable, that is, to protect lives and prevent crime.

In 1987, the Ministry of the Solicitor General and Department of National Defence agreed that DND would provide military assistance to support SERT, within the limits of Canadian Forces operational capability. An RCMP/DND memorandum of understanding followed. DND agreed to provide support to ensure the rapid deployment of SERT to resolve terrorist incidents at any location in Canada. This support includes, but is not limited to, the use of one CC-144 Challenger jet aircraft ready to depart within three hours of initial warning to DND, and one C-130 Hercules transport aircraft ready to depart within six hours of initial warning to DND.

DND may also provide assistance to SERT in the form of naval vessels, aircraft, armoured vehicles, communications and logistical support, as well as any other support requested by the RCMP. DND and the RCMP maintain a joint counter-terrorism capability and work together to ensure coordination of effort and to maintain the standards required of SERT. For example, DND pilots are trained to fly at low altitudes that may be required to deploy members of SERT at strategic locations.

Another MOU is now under development with DND, which could assist the RCMP in responding to terrorist crises. It involves law enforcement maritime preventative patrols. Under this agreement, RCMP officers would work off DND vessels to enforce preventative patrol in areas of Canadian jurisdiction. It is important to keep in mind that Canadian offshore waters cover some 6,500,000 square kilometres. The preventative patrols would be secondary tasking for DND, however, as military resources would be subject to national defence or search and rescue priorities. The locations for the patrols, as well as the number of ship days to be allotted, would be decided upon in advance, so as to synchronize DND and RCMP schedules.

This agreement will provide an RCMP presence in the patrol areas and assist in enforcing small vessel and other regulations, such as the Canadian Environmental Protection Act and other regulations related to environmental and wildlife protection. It will also provide a flexible response to criminal marine activity, which would include terrorist activity. The MOU could help control weapons smuggling by criminal extremists and aid in stopping criminal extremists attempting to enter the country illegally by sea.

DND could provide operational support for suppressing terrorist acts and apprehending those committing terrorist acts at sea, within Canadian waters. In order to support the preventative patrols, DND would provide ships' boats, including Rigid Inflatable Boats or Zodiacs, manned with appropriate DND crew, to conduct patrols at sea or in harbour.

Although this MOU has yet to be finalized, preliminary DND/RCMP patrols have already taken place. In addition, Maritime Patrol Aircraft are being used to assist in compiling surface plots of patrol areas. You will note that this agreement, as well as the one providing assistance for SERT, augment protective security measures for internationally protected persons, which are the responsibility of the RCMP.

Assistance to Civil Authorities

So far, I have looked at how the military assists the RCMP in its drug enforcement and counterterrorism role. Assistance to the police is also given in other crisis situations, from search and rescue missions to natural disasters. Much of this type of aid falls under the category of assistance to civil authorities.

Assistance to civil authorities would be given in the event of nuclear accidents, floods, earthquakes, explosions, fires, severe storms, or any event involving danger to lives or property, in which police resources are deemed insufficient. Military aid could include supplying food, medical services and emergency shelters, as well as transportation for evacuation operations.

Crisis situations that require military assistance to civil authorities could also be man-made. For example, a terrorist group attacking power lines might cause blackouts in major metropolitan areas for extended periods of time. Attacks on nuclear facilities could also cause emergency situations. I have already mentioned the activities of Direct Action, whose members were convicted of bombing a British Columbia hydro station and a Litton Industries Building in Toronto in 1982.

Groups that advocate terrorist activities in support of various political causes pose a potential threat to the safety of people and the environment on a mass scale. The damage caused by Direct Action was limited. We have no way of knowing, however, if future terrorist incidents will not cause even more widespread danger to the security, safety and health of Canadians.

Indeed, as international terrorism has become more spectacular and destructive, the possibility cannot be discounted that terrorists could use nuclear, biological and chemical agents to further their cause. In fact, to cope with such potential threats, a special group was formed, known as the Special Threat Assessment Group, or STAG. STAG is activated by the Solicitor General of Canada and is represented by DND, as well as various medical, scientific and security experts. STAG's primary role is to assist government and law enforcement officials.

Among its responsibilities are: assessing the magnitude of threats and the consequences of their execution; identifying the medical and physical resources required to cope with potential threats; and coordinating federal assistance in order to cope with problems of rescue, relief and evacuation, in the event of terrorist incidents involving nuclear, biological or chemical agents. DND would of course be heavily involved in all of these functions. As well, in the event of such occurrences, DND could be called in under Federal Emergency legislation or assistance to civil authorities.

Aid to Civil Powers

Separate from the category of assistance to civil authorities is the category of aid to civil powers. Aid to civil powers could be given by the military during times of political or social crisis. In cases of riots or disturbances of the peace, for example, the military can be called in if the power of the civil authorities is deemed insufficient to contain or resolve the situation. This type of assistance implies armed response and is normally obligatory on the part of the military. It should be mentioned that while the police do have well equipped specialized units, they can run into problems in cases where efforts must be sustained over long periods of time. Such conditions are always a drain on operational resources.

You will recall two notable examples of aid to civil powers which occurred during the past few decades. The first was during the October crisis in 1970, and the second, more recent example, occurred during the Oka crisis in the summer of 1990. In both cases, police resources were supplemented with military resources for the purposes of restoring law and order. Military officers took on the civilian peace officer role of the police. This of course left the police able to attend to their regular law enforcement duties of conducting criminal investigations and prosecuting criminal offences.

Aboriginal Crisis of 1990

Still fresh in your memories, I am sure, are the unsettling events of 1990 that resulted in the military being called into Quebec to resolve the standoff at Oka and at the Mercier Bridge. In addition, on the Akwasasne reserve near Cornwall, Ontario, the military's aid was requested twice. In fact, at Akwasasne, legitimate leaders and residents of the reserve, who were faced with heavily armed persons exercising power through violence and intimidation, approached government officials and stated that they were in fear of their lives. In the spring of 1990, military aid was requested through civil law enforcement agencies to support the police presence there.

A few months later, the military were called back, this time specifically tasked to evacuate police and equipment from the reserve, should it be deemed necessary. Meanwhile, the military were also called in to assist in dismantling the illegal roadblock at the Mercier Bridge, and to restore public order.

It should be stated that in these incidents DND assistance was not limited to restoring law and order. Civilian police forces, consisting of the Quebec Police Force, the Montreal Urban Community Police, the Ontario Provincial Police and the RCMP, received other forms of assistance. These included surveillance and technical communications and logistical support, as well as intelligence sharing. Logistical support included such things as transportation, food, bullet-proof vests, heaters and medical services.

As far as intelligence sharing was concerned, joint intelligence groups, which included members from the RCMP and DND were established at police command posts at Oka, Chateauguay and Cornwall. In addition, a military liaison officer was posted at the Quebec RCMP Division Emergency Operations Centre, to facilitate special requests related to both logistics and intelligence.

We hope the events of the spring and summer of 1990 will not be repeated. Unfortunately, harmonious relations in any community are not guaranteed. As a society we are all responsible for working together to prevent social alienation and discord.

Yet, when problems lead to illegal and violent occurrences and the breakdown of civil authority, the police and the military, which are the only sectors of society entitled by law to use force, and even then only to the extent that is considered reasonable, will inevitably be called in to deal with the situation.

We must be mindful of the possibility of such events and be fully informed of potential crisis situations. Continued intelligence sharing with the military is therefore necessary, both to prevent and prepare for such situations. Also, intelligence sharing, for such purposes as drug enforcement and counterterrorism, enables the RCMP and other police forces to be more proactive. It helps us develop long-term strategies to reduce criminal offences.

The logistical support we receive from DND is also necessary, for as I hope I have demonstrated, it has helped us many times and in many ways to do our job. As I mentioned earlier, the challenges facing the police have become increasingly diverse and complex, and our economic and personnel resources are increasingly limited. Outside cooperation enables us to make the most of our resources, both financial and human. It allows us to better meet existing challenges, and to take on new ones.

Namibia

Before I conclude, I would like to give an example of one of the new challenges taken on by the RCMP, a challenge which would not have been feasible without DND assistance. It is also an example of how the principle of cooperation applies on an international scale.

In 1989, the RCMP went into Namibia to support the United Nations Transition Assistance Group to help monitor that country's free elections and its move to independence. RMCP officers acted in an observer-advisory capacity. They monitored and reported on the activities of SWAPOL, the Southwest African Police. DND provided much of the logistical support to the RCMP in this new role, from postal services and tropical clothing, to equipment for field operations. Should the RCMP go to the Western Sahara to perform civilian policing duties as part of a United Nations Peacekeeping Mission, and should UN duties become a regular function of RCMP activity, we foresee the need for continued support from DND.

Conclusion

In conclusion, I want to say again that cooperation is one of the most effective ways to meet the new challenges that confront us, both at home and across the world. Cooperation from the

Canadian military has been vital to the RCMP in many of its law enforcement roles, including drug enforcement and counterterrorism.

DND has also come to our aid in crisis situations involving the breakdown of civil power, taking on the civilian peace officer role of the police, so that we could resume our regular police duties. DND has even assisted the police community in supporting the transition to independence and democracy in another part of the world.

It is interesting that within the past few years we have seen the military take on the civilian peace officer role of the police, and the RCMP take on the peacekeeping role normally associated with the military. Perhaps, in the future we will see a further convergence of our respective roles. In any case, we look forward to continued cooperation with DND and to the prospect of meeting many challenges together.

Questions and Answers

Q. Vice Admiral Dan Mainguy

In my opinion, there has always been a distinction between the role of the policeman and that of the military man. The policeman's job is fundamentally to act on information received in a largely compliant society and bring alleged offenders before the courts. A military man's fundamental objective is to operate at the behest of his government to restore order in a society which is not necessarily compliant. It seems to me, from what you have said, that this distinction is beginning to blur. I would like get a sense of the policeman's view of this situation. Do you think that there is there any danger that this increased cooperation may lead to a sort of police state atmosphere?

A. The ultimate purpose of all of this activity is to bring criminals before the courts. Whatever techniques used to achieve this are examined and will be prohibited if they are found to be unconstitutional. We're not talking of the military taking on a 'police' role. Basically their role has been to provide support to the RCMP. In today's environment, in contrast to what happened years ago, new challenges to law enforcement, such as the Colombian drug cartels, cannot be met with large capital procurements. Today, we must be very economical with our use of resources. To combat these challenges we need ships and aircraft. The military has this equipment. It makes economic sense, therefore, for these organizations to coordinate their efforts and resources. Military support may be as simple as flying over a region and reporting to the RCMP that a particular ship is indeed the one we were interested in. They are not doing anything overt in the way of detaining, arresting or imprisoning people.

Q. Brigadier General William Yost

One of the responsibilities of the Solicitor General and the RCMP is the protection of the thousands of vital points in Canada. You mentioned this briefly, but it seems to me that this could be a major task of our Reserves if there was, in fact, a terrorist attack or some other disturbance across the country which affected large numbers of people. Could you elaborate on what you see as the tasking of the Canadian Forces in regard to that responsibility of the RCMP and whether we should be doing more training and planning for such an occurence?

A. In the area of vital points, and even in the protection of V.I.P.'s, everything we do is based upon threat assessments which are provided by a wide range of sources, including intelligence services. We allocate resources in terms of these threat assessments. I fully agree with you that it is physically impossible to protect every vital point in this country. Depending on the nature of the crisis, assistance could be anything from asking for help to physically locate individuals to the hiring of security guards. During the Gulf War we had contingency plans to ensure the protection of vital points, but fortunately the situation never deteriorated to that stage.

Q. Major General J.J.A. Doucet

In your introduction you made reference to the fine cooperation which started the association between the RCMP and the military. If I may, I would like to make the specific observation that A Battery Kingston and B Battery from Quebec formed the nucleus of the North West Mounted Police. That said, I will now pose my question. In your address you stated that military assistance enables the specialist officers to concentrate on their proper role of investigation. It may be treading on delicate ground, given that the charges following the incidents at Oka are now before the courts, but I would like to refer to the disclosures of these cases, which would lead laymen to believe that there was a regrettable lack of foundation in some of the charges that were laid. Would you comment on the particular difficulties in presenting valid or substantiated charges, based on what we, the public, have seen or heard during that period.

A. The question of evidence is always an issue for the courts to determine. As police officers, it is our job to bring a case to the courts and the job of the judiciary to make the decision of admissability.

Q. Shane Henry

I would like to return to your comments regarding the RCMP contribution to the UN operation in Namibia and possible further involvement in UN peacekeeping. Is it the intent of the force to deal with these as they arise or are you doing contingency planning in terms of your own capabilities and potential areas of liaison with DND?

A. A fundamental tenet of law enforcement is that police can only function in a stable environment, in other words, where the majority of the population accept the fact that there is a role for the police. Our position is to look at each instance on a case-by-case basis and see if it is possible to put police in that particular environment.

IV

The Future of
Arms Control

by
Brigadier General B.A. Goetze
Director General
International Policy Operations

When reflecting about the state of international relations, I think even the most casual observer would agree that we have just entered a new chapter in world history. In the history books of the future, the chapter entitled "The Cold War" will end with references to the fall of the Berlin Wall, the collapse of the Soviet Union, and the end of bipolar East-West confrontation. We know that these events are a turning point in world history. But looking ahead, what do we see? A lot of people assumed that the next chapter in the history books of the future would have titles like "The Age of Arms Control". That is because arms control has played such an important and prominent role on the international stage in the past few years, and has contributed to the overhaul of the entire system. Because of its importance, many have assumed that arms control would be a growth industry until at least the end of the millennium. And yet, there are signs on the horizon that arms control as we have come to know it may not survive the upheavals of the late 1980's and early 1990's.

What I intend to do today is to briefly outline the effect that dramatic changes in the strategic environment have had on recent arms control agreements, and then to discuss what I believe will be the most important and productive components of arms control in the future. But first, I think it may be useful to define what is meant by arms control.

By arms control, I mean either the regulation of the size and development of military forces, or the prohibition of the development or use of particular weapons. Such regulation or prohibition is normally achieved through some form of formal agreement or treaty. Because there is no way for international law to enforce such agreements or treaties, they must not be seen as substitutes for a sound security policy. Indeed, in the absence of trust and the political will to cooperate, existing arms control treaties are little more than scraps of paper — or perhaps worse, a dangerous delusion of security. On the other hand, when there is adequate trust and the political will to cooperate, formal treaties of this type can be useful instruments of stability and bring about real reductions in armaments. Equally important, the negotiating process itself helps to open up channels of communication between adversaries. That in itself may be vital to handling the sorts of problems which we may see emerging in the new world order.

Let me now turn to a brief outline of what I believe has been the major effect of the end of the Cold War on recent arms control agreements.

It is a paradox that, in the past few years, arms control agreements which had been under negotiation for a very long time were being finalized just at the moment when many of the Cold War problems those agreements sought to address were disappearing at an ever-increasing pace. The most obvious Cold War problem which arms control was meant to address was the overwhelming Soviet conventional and nuclear threat. When the Cold War was at its height, it was imperative to reduce the asymmetries in the military balance favouring the Soviet Union. Unfortunately, attempts to negotiate reductions throughout the seventies and early eighties which would minimize Soviet conventional offensive power were unsuccessful. Indeed, our major successes have been achieved just as the Cold War was coming to an end: The Conventional Forces in Europe Treaty (CFE), signed in November 1990, was an agreement among the 22 nations of NATO and the former Warsaw Pact to dramatically reduce conventional weaponry in Europe. The Warsaw Pact had already begun to disintegrate by the time the treaty was signed, complicating the problems of deciding which countries would be able to keep the quotas which had been divided according to the two alliances. These problems are all the greater now that the Warsaw Pact has disappeared and the Soviet Union has broken apart.

Negotiating reductions in the nuclear weapons of the two sides was equally time-consuming and difficult. Despite progress in the strategic arms limitation treaties of putting ceilings on the number of strategic nuclear weapons to be held by the Soviet Union and the United States, the multiplication of nuclear warheads continued unabated. As in the case of conventional arms control, nuclear arms control has achieved success very late in the Cold War. Although there were notable earlier successes — such as the removal of intermediate-range nuclear weapons in the INF Treaty of 1987 — the Strategic Arms Reduction Treaty was signed only six months before the collapse of the Soviet Union. We now have four republics with strategic nuclear weapons on their territories, where before we had only one. We cannot underestimate the difficulties which will be faced in implementing an agreement signed by the Soviet Union, but which we now seek to have implemented by Russia, Ukraine, Belarus, and Kazakhstan.

The major effect of the dramatic events in central and eastern Europe on the CFE and START Treaties has thus been to greatly dampen their significance. Indeed, even among those who recognize the continuing importance of arms control, there is an increasing scepticism about the value of negotiated agreements. In the place of agreements which can take years to negotiate, there has been a move toward unilateral declarations such as the announcements by President George Bush on 27 September 1991. This increased use of unilateralism comes largely from a sense of urgency that measures such as consolidating nuclear weapons and removing them from unstable areas cannot await lengthy negotiation. There is therefore an increased tendency to announce unilateral arms control measures while at the same time calling for the other side to reciprocate.

But while the new US approach to arms control has been called "reciprocal unilateralism", at least 50% of the proposals in the Bush initiative are relevant only in the context of traditional arms control *negotiations* as we have come to understand them. For example, the US proposal to negotiate a revision to the Anti-Ballistic Missile (ABM) Treaty would have required direct negotiations. Another example is the President's proposal that the United States and the former Soviet Union agree to eliminate all ICBMs with multiple warheads. Rather than announce a unilateral reduction, he offered to negotiate an agreement. My point here is that even the Bush initiative, which some have characterized as the end of the traditional negotiating approach to arms control, is itself full of references which imply its continuance. So it seems that what we have now is not the death of the traditional arms control approach, but rather an infusion of unilateralism designed to deal with new and rapidly changing circumstances where the old method seems too slow.

That being said, there are still a number of significant advantages to getting countries to sign formal arms control treaties.

First of all, signed agreements make it more difficult for the other side to suddenly change direction, and make it possible for other countries to lodge legitimate complaints if they do. If measures have been taken unilaterally by a government, there is no certainty that other governments will reciprocate.

A second reason why negotiated agreements have a continuing value is that detailed verification of these treaties can ease the task of confirming that agreed reductions or other measures have actually taken place. In contrast, unilateral measures require a great deal of trust, and can be easily misinterpreted because they lack the specificity of negotiated agreements. In that sense, they could actually diminish security by heightening a sense of suspicion about real military capabilities of potential adversaries.

Thirdly, negotiated agreements can channel reductions in directions which are most conducive to international stability, while unilateral cuts are more likely to be driven by economic imperatives or other domestic political considerations, and may even, in some cases be simply random.

So, where do we go from here? What then is the future of arms control? you may well ask. Naturally, we must first identify what the new objectives of arms control are. I would suggest that we have already seen some evidence of the new kinds of problems which we are going to face. We have the question of nuclear weapons control among the Soviet successor republics. We have the example of the violent break-up of Yugoslavia. And finally, we have the example of the Gulf War. If these current problems are any indication, the main challenge for arms control in the future will be with preventing weapons proliferation, and with enhancing regional stability.

In pursuit of regional stability, the most important arms control fora will be those limiting conventional forces, such as the CFE Treaty, and those which provide confidence-building measures in areas of tension or actual conflict.

Conventional East-West Arms Control and Regional Stability

As was implicit in my earlier discussion, the future of the CFE Treaty is very much in question. Canada is particularly concerned that the independent Soviet successor states are likely to have neither the resources nor the inclination to implement the treaty. The main reason for the CFE Agreement was to reduce the threat posed by Soviet and Warsaw Pact offensive capability against the West. Because this threat has largely disappeared, we must now decide whether the structures and limitations imposed by the CFE Agreement can serve our new objectives of regional stability and preventing arms proliferation. In terms of regional stability, the CFE structure may have a role to play in the limitation of the vast amounts of military equipment which is spread throughout the new republics. But if the CFE Agreement is to have this role, there seems little doubt that renegotiation will be necessary, so that each independent republic can feel assured that its own security needs have been met. Perhaps a good approach would be to persuade the new republics to accept the existing terms of the Treaty, and then begin more detailed discussion on how to implement them.

I believe it is important for the West to maintain the expectation among the new republics that defence matters are not just an internal matter, but are the concern of the international community as a whole. To that end, the implementation of the CFE Agreement can serve to reduce the arms which the republics could otherwise use against each other, and in doing so establish a working relationship which will be essential for progress when the political and economic situation is more settled. In many ways, implementation of the CFE Treaty will also have the characteristics of confidence building measures.

Confidence and Security-Building Measures

Even while we are wrestling with implementing existing arms control agreements, new ones are being negotiated. For example, new confidence building measures and limits on manpower are being negotiated in the CFE follow-on negotiations which are scheduled to end before March 1992. Canada and Germany have co-sponsored a draft agreement which will effectively place ceilings on the size of the armed forces of the 22 signatory countries by requiring any manpower increase to be justified to other signatories.

Once this follow-on treaty is in place, new negotiations will begin in Helsinki involving CFE negotiating parties and all members of the Conference on Security and Cooperation in Europe (CSCE). Before turning to these negotiations in Helsinki, I would like to touch briefly on the subject of the CSCE and the Vienna Document.

As most of you will know, the CSCE is Pan-European and is currently comprised of the 36 European states plus the United States and Canada. In January 1991, CSCE member states signed the *Vienna Document* which is aimed primarily at establishing confidence-building measures, such as allowing for the observation of military exercises of a certain size which have been announced well in advance.

The Helsinki Talks

The March 1992 Helsinki Conference will bring the CSCE and CFE processes together. Participants will seek agreement on security and stability at lower levels of armed forces; intensified security dialogue; a new quality of transparency and cooperation about armed forces and defence policies; and effective mechanisms and instruments for conflict prevention.

Given the immense problems which we now have in implementing existing agreements, the prospects for dramatic success in the Helsinki Talks is limited. Nevertheless, what may be most important here is to keep the dialogue going, so that further progress can be made once the internal political situation in the new republics is more stable.

Conventional Arms Proliferation

Up to this point I have concentrated on East-West arms control, and the problems which we face there. However, there are other areas of arms control where real progress is not only possible but imperative, most notably with respect to arms control in the third world. At the top of the list are the issues of arms transfers, biological and chemical weapons.

In the wake of the Cold War, there is a massive reserve of military equipment of all types, including conventional, nuclear, biological, and chemical weapons. Not only do these weapons have to be reduced in order to establish regional stability among the new republics, but efforts are needed to prevent these weapons from being sold beyond their borders. In this sense, the potential problems of proliferation arising out of the end of the Cold War are immense.

In addition to these new problems, we have the example of Iraq, where extensive development of nuclear and other types of weapons had outstripped any of our best predictions. As the example of Iraq has shown, if we are to prevent the proliferation of weapons, we are going to have to address the issues of arms transfers, and the verification of treaty obligations. The Iraqi example has illustrated that inspecting only declared sites leaves far too much leeway for clandestine development to take place at undeclared sites. This is a problem which applies equally to nuclear, chemical, and biological weapons.

Conventional Arms Transfers

The problem posed by the international arms trade has been most vividly illustrated by the war between Iran and Iraq, and secondly by the Iraqi invasion of Kuwait. If wars such as this are to be limited and their consequences minimized, then the flow of arms to such regions will require careful regulation. Towards the end of the Gulf War Canada announced a major initiative to limit international arms transfers. Soon after, British Prime Minister John Major called for the establishment of a universal register of arms sales to be supervised by the United Nations. The arms registry would include information on the international sale of heavy arms which can be used to seize and hold territory such as battle tanks, armoured combat vehicles, combat aircraft, attack helicopters, warships and missiles or missile systems. Member states would provide information about imports and exports of arms as well as "other interrelated information" such as information on current military holdings and relevant national policies.

Furthermore, at the end of the London Summit of the G-7 in July 1991, the participating countries published a "Declaration on Conventional Arms Transfers and Nuclear/Biological/Chemical Non-Proliferation". The declaration noted that many states depend on arms imports, but it also distinguished this dependence from the threat to international stability caused by the accumulation of "a massive arsenal that goes far beyond the needs of self defence." The declaration asserted that this could be prevented by the application of the three principles of *transparency, consultation and action.*

All of the heavy arms I noted above are in fact covered in the CFE Agreement, with the exception of warships and missiles or missile systems. The issue of controlling missile technology is now being covered in the Missile Technology Control Regime (MTCR). This concern is partly a spin-off from the fear of nuclear proliferation, and is an attempt to prevent the spread of nuclear delivery capability. The control of warships is more controversial and is an issue to which I will turn shortly.

Chemical and Biological Weapons

While our objectives with regard to chemical and biological weapons have not changed, some of the challenges we face in implementing effective agreements in this area may have changed. Canada is particularly supportive of verification regimes which maximize information on national programs, thereby minimizing the likelihood of clandestine programs. As with conventional weapons programs, our difficulties in the area of chemical and biological weapons have been complicated by the break-up of the Soviet Union. The risk of the spread of these weapons is particularly formidable when one considers their potential utility to aggressors in regional conflicts, and the relatively easy access to weapons components. Control of chemical and biological weapons is therefore a high arms control priority for the coming year.

Nuclear Arms Control

As with conventional arms control agreements, the main short-term objective of nuclear arms control negotiations is to get the Soviet successor republics to honour the agreements which have already been signed. In this regard, of course, we have the bilateral US-USSR Strategic Arms Reduction Treaty (START) which was signed in July 1991. With the distribution of the Soviet strategic arsenal among four newly independent republics, implementing the agreement will pose immense difficulties.

We need to ask, however, whether there are not more pressing problems to deal with than those addressed by the START agreement, which is mainly aimed at maintaining strategic stability. At a time when the unity of command for the strategic nuclear forces of the former Soviet Union is very much in doubt, ideas of strategic stability begin to lose their primacy. Perhaps once the situation stabilizes and the command and control of nuclear weapons has been clarified by the government of the new republics, attention can then be refocussed on strategic stability as the main objective of nuclear arms control.

The more pressing issue for the international system today is the threat of nuclear proliferation. While this issue has been a critical one almost since the invention of nuclear weapons, what has made the threat more immediate is the exacerbation of traditional proliferation problems by the demise of the central control exercised by the former Soviet Union and by the elimination of the constraints imposed by what used to be an essentially bipolar world.

As is now well known, the United Nations Special Commission (UNSCOM) in Iraq has discovered that, prior to the Gulf War, Iraq's nuclear programme was far more advanced than had been predicted by even the most alarmist of worst-case scenarios. Had the 1981 Israeli attack on an Iraqi nuclear reactor, and the 1991 Gulf War, not taken place, Iraq would almost certainly be a nuclear power today. At the same time, US intelligence recently concluded that North Korea, one of the most heavily armed and isolated countries in the world, would likely be capable of producing weapons grade plutonium as early as mid-1992, and nuclear weapons by mid-1993. As in the case of Iraq, this is much earlier than previously thought. While Iraq's capability appears to have been effectively neutralized, it remains to be seen whether a New Year's Eve declaration by North and South Korea not to "test, produce, receive, possess, store, deploy, or use nuclear weapons" has halted the North Korean programme. In addition to these more dramatic examples, a host of other nations — including Israel, South Africa, India, Pakistan, Brazil, Argentina, Algeria, Iran and Libya — are all at various stages along the spectrum of nuclear capability.

The demise of the Soviet Union has produced, almost overnight, four new nuclear powers where there was once only one. According to US estimates, while most of the 27,000 Soviet nuclear warheads are deployed within the Russian Republic, nearly 5,000 tactical warheads and several thousand strategic warheads are scattered across Ukraine, Belarus, and Kazakhstan. In an area of the world where there is substantial political, economic and ethnic unrest, there could be catastrophic consequences if the ability to control these weapons fell into the wrong hands. The prospect of a "nuclear Yugoslavia", as enunciated by the American Secretary of State and others, formed the basis of the American and European Community policy that former Soviet republics would not be recognized without assurances that all former Soviet nuclear arms would be placed under centralized control. While Russia, Ukraine, and Belarus have issued such assurances, Kazakhstan's position is not yet clear.

Perhaps more worrisome than the proliferation of nuclear weapons within the former Soviet Union, however, is the potential effect which the coincidence of Soviet economic deterioration with the end of the bipolar world may have on the proliferation of nuclear capability around the world. It is somewhat ironic to note that, in our increasingly interdependent world, the end of the superpower stand-off has had the effect of regionalizing power politics. Throughout the Cold War period, Third World nations could enjoy a certain degree of protection from a perceived or de facto regional threat simply by allying itself with one super-power against the other. With the end of the Cold War, regional enemies may now feel more compelled to develop their own nuclear insurance policy. Thus the Cold War thaw may have the long-term effect of increasing the regional demand for nuclear weapons.

At the same time the economic crisis within the former Soviet Union may result in an increased supply of nuclear weapons components, technology and expertise. Although Mr. Yeltsin has assured the outside world that there will be strict export controls over nuclear related material, harsh economic realities in the newly independent nuclear armed republics may make it difficult for him to fulfil this promise. The dismantling of nuclear weapons will free up key weapons components, including uranium and plutonium. It has been suggested that those with access to these components could be tempted to sell them — or an entirely reconstructed nuclear device — to various Third World nations for desperately needed hard currency. Already evidence of such practices have emerged: An Italian judicial official has stated that uranium confiscated in Zurich in November, and plutonium seized in northern Italy in December, were identified by US experts as being of Soviet origin. He further noted that the material was destined for countries using East Bloc technology, such as Iraq and Libya.

Equally worrisome is the possible spread of nuclear weapons technology and expertise. The Central Intelligence Agency has estimated that as many as 2,000 people in the Soviet nuclear weapons community have a detailed knowledge of nuclear weapons design, and 3,000 to 5,000 people have worked in uranium enrichment and plutonium production. High levels of unemployment in the former Soviet republics could prompt those with nuclear expertise to sell their skills and knowledge abroad to Third World countries aspiring to become nuclear capable. Obstacles faced by such countries could be more quickly overcome by employing nuclear scientists who have already solved the problems which these countries still face. Again, evidence of such job offers have already emerged. A senior scientist at Moscow's Institute of Atomic Energy has revealed that at least two of his colleagues had received high-paying job offers from Libya. Although the offers were for work only on peaceful uses of atomic energy, and in any case were turned down, this scientist readily acknowledged that the two experts' skills could easily be applied to nuclear weapons. It may only be a matter of time before offers are accepted out of economic necessity.

Thus the political and economic demise of the Soviet Union, coupled with the definitive end of the bipolar world, has dramatically increased the threat of nuclear proliferation. The fact that this threat serves to further compound what was already a critical international issue has made the proliferation of nuclear capability the most crucial issue of the international system today. The challenge for the future is to determine what action must be taken in order to sufficiently address this issue. The Bush Administration has called for the creation of a nuclear-free Middle East and Korean Peninsula. A first step in this process would be to make all governments sign the nuclear Non-Proliferation Treaty (NPT) and put their facilities under the safeguards of the International Atomic Energy Agency (IAEA). However the experience with Iraq — an NPT signatory which submitted to IAEA safeguards — has made it clear that the NPT needs to be stiffened and that existing IAEA provisions are insufficient. NPT signatories must work toward an agreement to extend the IAEA's area of operation from declared to undeclared (and suspected) nuclear sites. At the same time, increased international pressure must be applied to those countries which have so far refused to sign the NPT.

Conclusion

Allow me now to summarize. In my view, arms control has an important and necessary part to play in future international security and stability. With the demise of the Soviet Union, however, the main thrust of arms control will no longer be toward bilateral or bloc to bloc agreements but rather toward regional and multilateral treaties. While there will be value in unilateral measures, there will continue to be clear advantages to negotiated agreements of the more traditional kind. Our efforts will have to be particularly pragmatic on this point, especially when dealing with the new republics. In some cases all we can expect is to keep other countries engaged in the dialogue in order that we may be able to achieve more practical measures once the political situation stabilizes. Additionally, we will have to pay special attention to controlling conventional arms transfers and nuclear proliferation in the future if we are to prevent a recurrence of the same sort of clandestine build-up that we witnessed in Iraq.

What I have outlined for you today suggests that there is a lot of work ahead for those of us engaged in arms control, and we should not overlook either the difficulties we face, or underestimate the necessity of achieving our objectives. Whether the context is East-West, North-South, nuclear, conventional, biological, chemical, unilateral, bilateral, or multilateral, viable arms control arrangements may well be the key to peace and the foundation of a new world order.

From the Canadian perspective there is much to be gained from a process of dialogue. Even if in the short term we have difficulties reaching agreements, the process of negotiation itself can give us insights which can lead to the growth of trust. I believe that at the root of our continuing arms control efforts must be the recognition that the security of nations is an international matter which is best worked out through cooperation, consultation, and the conclusion of agreements which enhance stability at the lowest possible level of armaments.

Questions and Answers

Q. Bill Hillaby, Navy League of Canada

One aspect of arms control over the past many years has been that of naval arms control. In view of the break up of the Soviet Union and, indeed, evidently of their fleets, what, in your view, is the outlook for improved progress in the matter of naval arms control and if there is any, along what line?

A.

The subject of naval arms control has been broached consistently throughout the last 10 or 15 years, mostly by the former Soviet Union. Principally it was directed at trying to constrain the freedom of movement of the United States Navy as a strategic nuclear navy alongside its significant conventional capability. Canada has taken the approach on naval arms control that, as a minimum, one ought to start to talk about the negotiation of some confidence building measures. That is to say, measures which would require a certain degree of pre-notification of activities close to the proximity of countries and so on. I am not aware that the US Navy has softened its stand on this particular issue, and I must add that there are other NATO allies, such as France and the United Kingdom, who have taken a similar position: that until such time as a regime can be devised which would not restrict the freedom of navigation or movement on the seas, I don't think that we're going to make any significant progress in negotiating naval arms control agreements. That being said, I think it is interesting that, not only have there been significant unilateral reductions by countries in ground and air forces, but we read almost daily of reductions in naval forces. The question, of course, will arise: Will there be some point in the future where we can codify these reductions into some sort of understanding. I think that remains to be seen. There is greater recognition of the need to address the area of naval arms control, but I don't see in the immediate future any steps to actually try to put this down in some sort of treaty.

Q. David Code, CDA Institute

You have given us much to be fearful of, and one of the most frightening is the vast numbers of Soviet-trained people who have this knowledge which could prove mischievous and who, at the same time, are desperately short of the means of making a living. This is brought into sharper focus by this week's news that the Iranians are anxious to expand their influence into the Islamic republics, including Kazakhstan, which is a nuclear power. Has anyone given any thought to trying to solve both problems by having an international agency, the United Nations for example, create an institute which would offer to hire these people as a means of keeping them from getting loose.

A. The problem is that it would take an incredible amount of money. There are a lot of people, particularly in some of the countries I made reference to, who have access to financial resources with which it would be very difficult to compete. While your idea is certainly one which could be considered, I think we have to first focus our efforts towards exposing and monitoring those nations which may be building a significant military capability. We need to make it clear to those countries that the international community will not tolerate the appearance of regional powers armed with these types of weapons systems. That may not be the most hopeful indication of how to deal with this problem but, as we saw in the interdiction that was launched against Iraq, they have been set back, they have been exposed, and we can now say that they are perhaps 5, 10, or 15 years away from where they were at the time of the interdiction. How we deal with the scientists, frankly, I'm not certain, other than to appeal to them that the world will be a much more dangerous place were they to sell their wares in the bazaars of the scientific community.

Q. Colonel Murray Johnston, Vice Chairman Ontario

You have spent a lot of time discussing the security aspects of arms control. Would you make a few comments on the environmental and safety aspects of arms control.

A. Clearly there are major concerns, particularly in the Soviet Union, regarding the handling of nuclear material. We are well aware of the Chernobyl disaster, and the inspections of some of the Soviet peaceful reactors have shocked Western scientists. There are major difficulties and concerns about the dismantling and destruction of nuclear weapons in accordance with established agreements, and what will happen to those fissionable materials. Equally, the dismantling of chemical and biological weapons is an area of considerable concern. Canada has offered, and indeed in the Iraq scenario has sent, scientists to try to deal with this, not only to identify the problems but also to assist in their destruction. I think there is a greater awareness of the environmental consequences of the storage and handling of nuclear materials, but there is a tremendous education process that must take place. The United States has offered to send nuclear experts to the Soviet Union, and indeed some of them are there. The Soviet Union up to this point, certainly the Russian Republic, has cooperated with those scientists in trying to develop methods of handling, dismantling and eventually disposing of these materials. There are some hopeful signs, but the challenge is enormous.

V

Progress in Making
a Total Force

by
Lieutenant General J.C. Gervais
Commander, Mobile Command

It is a distinct pleasure and honour to have this opportunity to speak to you in this forum. I believe that it is most appropriate, especially during these difficult times, that you be brought up to date on the challenges facing the army in order that you can focus your energies in helping us to sustain an operationally capable defence structure. As you aware, we will very shortly have a smaller regular army and a larger, more capable militia. This shift in balance in force strengths, however, does not necessarily equate to a loss of potential. By refocusing our priorities, we will be able to sustain an effective capability, as our efforts will be concentrated on the essential tasks at hand.

My aim in this address is to give you an overview of the progress we have made, and the challenges we are facing, in creating the Total Force Army of the future. I will be as frank and as unambiguous as possible in presenting my personal assessment, and I daresay that some of you may not totally agree with my observations. That difference of opinion is one of the challenges I have to face, but I welcome it, as there are times when we who work the problems day to day get too close to them and need to be reminded of easily overlooked aspects.

By way of background, one can trace the genesis of the army of the next century to the 1987 White Paper. At that time, we were planning to build a force called 'Army 2002', and considerable staff effort went into creating it. With the demise of the White Paper due to rapid and profound changes in the geo-strategic situation, we retained the concept of Army 2002, but modified it to reflect the emerging new world order and current fiscal restraints and limitations. There are a number of imperatives, led by the notion of Total Force, which together, if satisfied, will give the army a general purpose combat capability. This capability, in turn, will position the army to meet its objective which is, as stated, to be prepared for any contingency which may arise. I should add in passing that this vision is also applicable to the Air Force and Navy.

While I am a strong proponent of the concept of Total Force, the term itself has taken on a meaning of its own and, more often than not, it is seen as a threat to the existence of both the militia and regular force. In my opinion, this could not be further from the truth and I will elaborate on this later.

Our analysis of our future requirements has established three clear, simple themes that are being used to underpin our force development activities. The themes can be expressed in one phrase as follows: *A Total Force* Army with a *general purpose combat capability* operating within a *regional command structure*. It is important to link these themes together as they are interactive and shortcomings in addressing one dimension will weaken the other two. Conversely, development based on these themes will strengthen the army and support the new defence policy announced by the Minister last September.

Regional Structure

By way of example, let me review the unfolding of the *regional command structure*. Land Force Central Area and Land Force Western Area, headquartered in Toronto and Edmonton respectively, are in place and are exercising command and control of area resources through a unified chain of command. This is, I believe, most significant. The Area Commanders, one of whom, Major General Nick Hall, is a militia officer, exercise command over both regular and reserve units and formations in their areas. Their prime responsibility is force generation. To execute this task they are responsible for resources, training facilities and activity rates of both components, and will ensure that the appropriate emphasis and standards are achieved. This coordination was only present at Army HQ level before the Areas were formed, and our efforts were too often a mix of broad policy concerns and over-management of detail. The Areas are proving that no longer will the regulars and militia be 'two solitudes' operating with their own agendas.

The mindset of the separate entities, however, will take time to change since we are essentially influencing behaviours that have developed over decades. Progress will be measured in small steps.

Regardless of what I or any other commanders say, there will still be a tendency for either component to see the other as a threat to its existence and way of life. The regular force fear a dilution of quality, training standards and operational readiness, while the militia suspect that the regular force will overpower it and undermine the legacy and heritage of its history in the name of efficiency and cost-effectiveness. These suspicions are deep-seated and, although we attempt to minimize their influence, they are real and need to be addressed.

The regional command structure is a major development and, over time, will prove to be a critical element in all of our undertakings. We have had a glimpse of the future with LFCA and LFWA, and later this year Secteur de l'Est de la Force Terrestre and Land Force Atlantic Area will come into existence. As well, in April, Land Force Northern Area will be instituted, thereby providing an integrated command structure from sea to sea to sea. Northern Area, it must be noted, will be different from its southern brothers due to its more national role. Additionally, it will have fewer assigned resources and a minimal force generation capability, except for the Canadian Rangers and any future program to establish an aboriginal militia.

FMCHQ is also undergoing a metamorphosis that will lead it to focus on three principal functions, namely, policy, plans and resource allocation. The micro-management of recent years will be replaced with a new mindset — that of a National Army

Headquarters. The formation of the Area HQs will facilitate this transformation.

Therefore, from an organizational point of view we are getting our act together. There are obviously lessons to be learned, and challenges to be overcome, but I am convinced, now more than ever before, that we are following the proper course of action.

General Purpose Combat Capability

The second theme that we are addressing actively is the maintenance of a *general purpose combat capability*. This requirement is critical if Canada is to retain armed forces capable of supporting foreign policy commitments such as NATO and peacekeeping, as well as any domestic requirements. The effects of instituting this theme will have a dynamic influence over a broad range of programs ranging from equipment procurement to personnel policies.

We have determined that the army needs to retain its ability to function effectively across the spectrum of conflict, from low level operations to a mechanized scenario such as was seen in the Persian Gulf. To do this we need to retain our ability to mount, deploy, and sustain balanced formations which are competent in all combat functions. I emphasize that this is an army requirement, in which both the regular and militia components have a vital role to play.

A general purpose combat capability can also be seen as a compromise which acknowledges the art of the possible, guards against losing sight of professional imperatives and concentrates on achievable aims. In realizing this objective, we will require a disciplined approach to training and equipping the army. Again, the regional command structure will assist us immensely in sustaining this general purpose capability.

Organizationally, we will have to manage effectively the transition from here to 1995/96, given our reduction of forces in Europe, the downsizing of the regular force, the increase in the reserve force and the infrastructure adjustments. Due to the intense pace of activities in the next four years, I consider this period to be critical in establishing a firm basis from which we can address long-term objectives.

Our collective goal should be to educate the policy makers that these reductions may in fact, not realistically emphasize the actual costs of realigning the regular/reserve mix. Any reduction or downward adjustment will tend to be seen in terms of dollar savings. This is not necessarily so, at least in the short term, since, as evidenced by the Minister's September statement, any downward change in the size of the regular force is offset by increases in the reserve. Regular strength will decline from 23,500 to about 20,500 over the next three years, while militia strength will increase from 22,000 to 29,000 in the next 10 years. The Total Force Army will in fact expand, not decline! This will obviously not be free of cost. The challenge will be to calculate the net cost when we are faced with a constantly changing fiscal playing field. The bottom line is not as distinct as many would like to believe.

Organizational change, however, is inevitable as we adjust our total strength. But, change will be required from both regulars and militia if we are to optimize our effectiveness. Both components will be studied under the same microscope and establishments will have to be rationalized to provide the appropriate officer/NCO/soldier mix to meet the tasks at hand. The size and numbers of units, for instance the creation of 10/90 battalions in three of the areas will, of necessity, come under close scrutiny. Our goal must be to create win/win circumstances directly related to tasks, roles, establishments and readiness. We will not cause change for its own sake.

In your FORUM magazine of early 1989, Professor Willett suggested in an article entitled "Heritage at Risk", that the militia was never intended to be efficient in peacetime, but to act as a symbol. Regretfully, the appropriateness of that sentiment has long since disappeared and the luxury it implies is no longer affordable. In a constructive, cooperative and objective manner, ways must be found to sustain our army heritage while at the same time producing an effective and efficient force structure.

Progress may at times be slow, but we must never lose sight of the aim.

On a separate but no less important plane, we are making significant progress in training to ensure that general purpose combat skills are learned, practised and shared by all ranks. We are making strong efforts to sustain the benefits we gained from EX ON GUARD 90 which saw some 11,000 reservists train alongside the regular force. Last year, although no national exercise was involved, area militia concentrations were extremely successful with attendance totalling approximately 10,000. Area concentrations will occur again this year when the principal army training event will be RV 92. We have identified a need for some 1,000 reservists to support the exercise but expect the late spring timing to affect participation. For the future we are adjusting the scheduling of our training to optimize militia participation.

An example of deliberate and fundamental change is the introduction of a common training period within the annual training cycles of both the regular force and militia. Beginning in 1993, the regular force training cycle will be adjusted to create a collective training window in mid to late August when the regular force and militia will train together. Activities throughout the year will be adjusted accordingly in order that this period will be seen as the culmination of training.

In establishing such a period, a long standing desire to enhance training opportunities for the militia will be addressed. Expertise and resources will be shared and skills perfected within the appropriate scenario. In the first few years, the militia will concentrate on mastering individual skills and operations at the combat team level. Later, as capabilities increase, composite units and possibly formations may be formed and exercised by Area Commanders. The utility of the scarce resources allocated to both components will also be optimized.

But saying we will conduct this training and in fact doing it, are two very different things. For instance, we will have to closely manage the regular force annual posting season activities to ensure that soldiers are available for training. This will require the cooperation of many NDHQ agencies and even though resistance to change is expected, I am determined to follow through with my intent as a demonstrable example of how serious we are in making the Total Force Army work. Adjustments will also be needed to well-established training practices throughout the army, and these are currently being developed for appropriate staffing. Here I am referring to such things as participation on career courses for qualified members of both components of the army at appropriate levels.

As well, we are at work staffing several other initiatives that will underscore that the army needs to have a balanced look into the future. Among these projects are enhanced enrolment and training programs aimed at increasing the quality and quantity of militia NCOs. We know alternative programs are possible since we have successfully introduced the RESO structure for officers as an alternative to the lengthier militia training career profile. The challenge is to establish comparable programs for NCOs as the lack of options for training militia NCOs is critically affecting the ability of the militia to attain and sustain operational training standards. The length of time required to achieve NCO rank, and the extensive training, are both detractors. The aim is to streamline the process, but protect the quality line in order that militia service will become and remain attractive to prospective enrolees.

This will not, however, result in a single program to produce NCOs, as we recognize a requirement to appeal to a variety of individuals. Again, over time, the aim is to enhance and stabilize the militia NCO corps and make the militia more self-sufficient. In the interim, Land Force Areas will institute regular force/militia affiliations to make the necessary expertise available to militia units.

This idea of mutual support is best exemplified by what can be termed branch or corps training boards with the areas. In LFCA, and just now beginning in LFWA, these training boards have been created to ensure the application of training standards and the availability of training assistance. By delivering better focused training, we feel we will go a long way to meeting the soldier's requirements of interesting and challenging work, while concurrently raising our operational standards.

There are several other projects worth noting that are expected to positively influence general purpose combat training. These include the creation and distribution of some 38 training packages to militia units to assist instructors in preparing and delivering standardized training. As well, a series of instructional videos is in production for armoury and unit use.

We are also investigating ways to increase full-time support to militia units to approximately 10% of a unit's strength. This is aimed at reducing the routine administrative requirements of training nights, thereby freeing-up time for practical work in lieu of paperwork.

As well, throughout the army we are now addressing the need for modern, exciting training aids and simulators that can be employed in unit lines. A great portion of our training methodology is archaic and requires overhaul.

Although programs and initiatives are identified and being staffed, it would be false to believe that vast improvements will be evident overnight. Indeed, too rapid a change could be harmful and create unnecessary stress. But we must start by identifying the need for improvements, creating acceptable and affordable options and instituting the adjustments as part of a progressive program. This, I feel, is well underway.

I would like now to say a few words concerning the third variable of a general purpose combat capability, that of equipping the force. As is the case with our other programs, the underlying premise is that we will equip the entire army, making new equipment available to both components as necessary. As examples, new 10 ton heavy trucks will provide much needed lift and new light trucks are expected in 1993. New tactical radios, part of the TCCCS, IRIS system, are expected in 1994. It may well be that due to support or infrastructure limitations, the scales of issue will be different, but if we are to field one operational army, both components will have to have access to the necessary equipment.

The multi-role combat vehicle or MRCV will be available to the militia as well as to the regular force. Currently, we envisage a troop/platoon's worth in each unit armoury where practicable, and a small battle group's worth at each area training centre for collective training. Other capital projects such as laser-based, tactical engagement simulators will be available to both components for tactical field training.

It would be another false hope, I believe, to expect equal distribution of all new kit. Some equipment, such as improved targetry for training ranges, will benefit both components simply by being available. Other initiatives such as the procurement of a distributed learning capability via simulation will benefit primarily the militia, who will continue to function under particular constraints, principally time and dispersion.

It is significant, however, to hoist in the premise that no longer can we tolerate haves and have-nots within the army if we are to sustain our operational readiness and combat power. Accepting this thought, a great number of inappropriate and dysfunctional beliefs must be cast aside.

The sum total of maintaining a general purpose combat capability is therefore a closer operational weave between the two components of the army. By appropriately organizing, training and equipping the Total Force Army, we will be capable of responding to a complete array of possible military tasks.

Total Force

The last theme that I would like to address is that of Total Force itself. Historically, the Canadian Army has always been a total force, an army of two components varying in strength and capability depending on the world situation and our national agenda. The mixture of militia and regular forces, and without exception, a dedicated civilian component, has always been a hallmark of Canadian defence policy. This fact is just as true today as it was before World War II and our challenge is to shape the army of the future in order that it can be capable of responding to the country's needs.

Since the 1950's, however, Canada has maintained a relatively large standing army and has allowed the militia to languish. In retrospect, this was unfortunate. However, hindsight is only instructive if we apply its lessons to the future.

The events of the past 30 years or so have imprinted upon the current generation of officers a mindset that will be difficult to change. If we are not to repeat the failures of the past, the two components will have to forge a new partnership in which each is understood and accepted by the other; where similarities are emphasized and differences minimized; and where a new mutual cooperation is evident.

Today, I can safely tell you that we have gone beyond the *concept* of a Total Force; it is indeed becoming a *reality* in the army. The precepts that I have outlined are beginning to work and I am confident we will reap further dividends as these ideas mature.

To illustrate our modest success with an operationally capable militia, it should be noted that for the past two summers we have assigned a militia company under its own commander to security duties at the NATO Flight Centre at Goose Bay, Labrador. We have also had militia sub-units, again with their own commanders, serve in Cyprus along side their regular force counterparts. And, of course, we continue to employ excellent militiamen on an individual basis on most bases and in most headquarters. Some 600 militiamen also served well during Operation Salon, the native crises in 1990.

We have not overcome all of the challenges of Total Force to be sure, but we do have a good idea of the way ahead and we are making headway.

Summary

In as few words as possible, I have presented you with the progress we have made to date in moulding the army in which our sons and daughters will serve. Regardless of what we have accomplished, there is still a great deal of work to be done. I am convinced, however, that we are on the correct bearing and that if we are patient and view the small achievements as steps towards an institutional goal, we will achieve success and continue to provide Canada with an army of which she can be justifiably proud. The proportions of regular and militia may vary but our ultimate goal must always be an effective, professional army prepared for any contingency.

The task at hand is to sustain the momentum that we have created in realizing the three themes that I have described. To do this we need not only the best efforts of the regular and militia from within, but the support of the associations that make up the CDA. Your encouragement and counsel is most welcome and is counted upon to assist us over the bumps ahead.

In closing, let me assure you that the fundamental strength of the army continues to be the soldier. The army consists of good people. All ranks, and I specifically include the militia, have the spirit, enthusiasm and motivation to make the future army a proud descendant of its forebears. Our task is to provide the appropriate environment within which it can continue to evolve in a progressive manner.

Questions and Answers

Q. Brigadier General (Ret) W.J. Yost, CDA Institute

It is my understanding that attention is being given to assigning the militia service battalions specific roles, such as transport units or supply units. Does this mean that service battalions are to be — organizationally — changed back into something we had before?

A. This is one of the options being considered, but no presentation has yet been made to FMC.

Q. Tom Bauld

You spoke of the goal of "larger, more capable militia". In making this happen, how do you see the roles of the Chief of Reserves and DGRC in relation to the Command Headquarters?

A. An organization study is going on at NDHQ, but I expect there will not be much change within, say, the next five years, nor in that of the Chief of Staff, Reserves.

Q. George Bell

What can you tell us about the structures of the Brigade Groups?

A. There will be a training brigade in each of three areas.

Q. F.H.K. Krenz

Could you tell me how much cooperation we can expect from civilian employers?

A. General Mariage will be speaking on that subject during Friday's proceedings.

Q. Lieutenant Colonel Patrick

Based on my experience commanding 402 Squadron in Winnipeg, I feel that our big need is for more active reserves. Can you comment?

A. The U.S. Army Reserve, I know, does not attempt to train its reservists beyond the company level. But they are able to participate with the regulars and able to dedicate enough time to learn the skills. Their retention is fairly good, as is their readiness.

Q. Colonel Butson, Defence Medical Association

We have only one Canadian field hospital. Now in this country there are 197 emergency hospitals in moth-balls, and I am suggesting that the military should have access to them.

A. Yes. We want to get one or two in each area, for training use. But EPC (Emergency Planning Canada) does not want to release them — presumably for fear of the risk of damage).

Q. Lieutenant Colonel Jim Hubbell — Royal Canadian Artillery Association

Equipment will soon be available from Germany. Will some of it come to the Reserves, along with the "maintainers"?

A. I intend to see that happen, and I especially agree with your remark about the "maintainers".

Q. (Name not heard)

I would like to ask about the production of NCOs and the intake of recruits that is needed in order to yield the number of NCOs required?

A. I agree with your concern. In the past we relied on long-term reservists, but I am concerned that there may no longer be enough of them. Our problem lately has been with retention and for that reason we have been having to put more regulars in reserve units (when we can).

Editor's Note:

Some difficulty was experienced with the recording facility, so this question period has been reconstructed as well as human memory permits.

VI

Can the United Nations Assume a Peacemaking Role?

by
L. Yves Fortier
Former Canadian Ambassador
to the United Nations

From mid 1988 until very recently, I had the honour and privilege to represent Canada at the United Nations in New York. In 1989 and 1990 I was Canada's representative at the United Nations Security Council. I have thus witnessed first-hand what the UN can do to make this world a better place for all of us. I can also tell you without any hesitation that the UN I left a few weeks ago bore little resemblance to the UN I became accredited to in 1988. Nowhere in the organization have changes been more striking than in its peacemaking role, the timely subject of this conference.

Even for those of us who followed developments on a daily basis in the past few years, the changes have been dizzying. We are not only talking about an evolution in attitude, about an easier and more constructive dialogue among former adversaries; we are not only talking about increased cooperation and emergence of new prospects; we are talking about the rebirth of the United Nations, mirror of a new international society.

In the past few years, and increasingly, we have witnessed the disappearance of most traditional terms of reference, often with relief, but we have not found new ones which could really serve as a framework for international life in the nineties and the twenty-first century. Instead, we have acted in response to new and unpredictable circumstances, relying on the basic principles of the UN Charter and on some accepted international norms such as freedom and human rights, but often, inevitably, in an improvised way.

The results so far have, I think, been generally positive, but it remains true that no one today can honestly claim to see all the implications of events of the past few years, from Namibia to Western Sahara, from Nicaragua to Haiti, from Iraq to Cambodia, from the independent republics of the former Soviet Union to Yugoslavia. Tremendous energy will have to be spent in the next few years in weaving a new fabric for international relations, to ensure that the gains are consolidated, that global or regional chaos is avoided, and that the divide between the North and the South does not widen even further.

Where does peacemaking fit in to all of these changes, and what do we actually mean when we refer to a peacemaking role for the UN?

Peacemaking in the Classical Sense

Classically, at least at the UN, peacemaking has meant "diplomatic efforts", in a broad sense. The UN only became engaged in active peacemaking, in that sense, a few years ago when it became clear that the then superpowers were prepared, sometimes, to cooperate in establishing peace in certain regions, and at least sometimes to let peace be established by others, without imposing obstacles. It began quietly, in 1987, with the adoption of Resolution Number 598 by the Security Council which set out a series of measures aimed at settling the conflict between Iran and Iraq. This resolution was accepted by both parties one year later. Then we saw the adoption of a number of other plans in the subsequent two years, setting the foundation for peace in different regions: Namibia, Central America, Afghanistan, and Angola.

In many of those cases the lion's share of the work was done by the Secretary-General and his colleagues, sometimes pursuant to a specific mandate of the Security Council, sometimes at the request of the parties themselves. Sometimes though, the permanent members themselves contributed actively to the process, for example in the cases of Cambodia and Afghanistan. In any event, if today those activities are seen as run-of-the-mill for the organization, at the time they were nothing less than revolutionary.

To understand why, and to understand how startling other developments have been since then, it is necessary to fathom the rather tortuous evolution of the UN, and particularly its Security Council, since the foundation of the organization.

The declared objective of the drafters of the Charter was to grant the Council strong and centralized powers to deal with threats to and breaches of the peace and with acts of aggression. This was in part a reaction to the powers established in the covenant of the League of Nations, powers seen as woefully lacking. The Council's main powers are defined in Chapter VII of the UN Charter. It may call upon the parties to a conflict to comply with provisional measures, it may use measures not involving the use of armed force, including economic sanctions and, if these measures are inadequate, it may authorize "action . . . as may be necessary", involving the use of armed force. In other words, enforcement action. Its decisions are binding on all states.

This system, of course, could work only if the members of the Security Council, and particularly its permanent members who have a right of veto on substantive matters, achieved a large measure of cooperation. This did not happen for a long time. The permanent members, in keeping with the spirit of the Cold War, had major and prolonged disagreements in a variety of areas and used their veto frequently. Sanctions were rarely applied. The only military operation authorized by the Council was Korea, because at the time the USSR was boycotting the Council and was therefore not in a position to use its right of veto. This was an aberration which is unlikely ever to repeat itself. In other words, the Security Council in those years was largely ineffective. This was not the fault of the United Nations but rather of its member states. As we know, the United Nations is not a supranational government: It cannot impose solutions but rather, if allowed by its members, it can offer certain mechanisms which again can be effective only to the extent that states are willing to use them.

For the past few years the Council has played a more productive and constructive role than ever before. As I mentioned earlier, this is due to a large extent to the relaxation of tensions between Moscow and Washington, and to more general changes in the attitude of many states, with less emphasis on ideology and confrontation, more focus on economic and social problems and more interest in cooperation and the search for pragmatic solutions.

While there remain situations where the Council has been unable so far to act effectively — the Arab-Israeli conflict and the Palestinian issue are cases in point — there is no question that, in the past few years, the Council, more and more often, has been successful in setting up mechanisms which have assisted in ensuring a lasting peace in situations of conflict. I am still talking about peacekeeping, but a new and improved peace-keeping.

Peacekeeping operations began in the late forties, but they were considerably expanded and transformed some forty years later. To give you a telling figure, in its first 43 years the Security Council created 13 peacekeeping or observer missions. In the past four years, it has created nine more, many of them with much broader objectives that just interposing UN blue helmets between belligerents. Peacekeeping today involves the return of refugees, supervision of elections, humanitarian assistance, main-tenance of law and order and now, even monitoring of human rights. In other words, peacekeeping with a good dose of peacemaking.

The most recent peacekeeping or observer missions have been sent to the Middle East, Asia, Africa and Central America, with their functions as diverse as their deployment. In Afghanistan, UMGOMAP was designed to verify the withdrawal of Soviet troops from that country. UNAVEM I did the same with Cuban troops in Angola. UNAVEM II is now overseeing the ceasefire between the government of Angola and UNITA, and may well assume an election monitoring role too. UNIIMOG was created to supervise a ceasefire between Iran and Iraq which still holds, while UNIKOM provides a UN demilitarized zone between Iraq and Kuwait.

UNTAG, the Namibian operation, represented a more complex, more ambitious and more difficult operation. It had been on the books for over a decade and eventually managed the transition of Namibia to independence. The current operation in the Western Sahara, MINURSO, will eventually be on a similar scale.

Meanwhile, in Central America, ONUCA is designed to verify certain commitments undertaken by the five Central American governments in pursuit of regional peace and security. The Central American operation is in some ways the most interesting because it has taken on many diverse tasks, of an international and internal character, without in any way being linked to a situation of decolonization. The Security Council also established a separate operation in El Salvador, ONUSAL, the first phase of which consists of monitoring the human rights situation in that country.

ONUSAL is, in many respects, a unique departure for the Security Council. Originally intended to oversee a comprehensive settlement in El Salvador, this operation was in fact deployed in stages. The first stage monitored compliance with a human rights accord between the government and the FMLN. This was requested by both parties as a confidence building measure to support negotiations on the other aspects of a settlement agreement. Despite its reticence to involve itself in the internal affairs of a member state or to broaden its mandate beyond traditional areas of competence, the Security Council overcame its resistance in this specific case and is now monitoring human rights totally within the territory of one member state, something that would have been unthinkable little more than a year ago. Such action supported the more traditional peacemaking role of the Secretary-General and helped create a climate conducive to the negotiation of the comprehensive settlement that was signed in New York on New Year's Eve. Once the final details have been worked out, the Security Council is expected to approve the deployment of the other stages of ONUSAL, including the more traditional military observers.

Perhaps the most extensive and complicated UN peacekeeping operation to date, in terms of scope and size, is represented by the Cambodia operation — UNTAC. UNTAC, as elaborated in the Paris Conference on Cambodia last October, involves direct UN participation in a wide variety of activities including interim civil administration of key government ministries, repatriation of Cambodian refugees and displaced persons, elections monitoring, and a wide range of military matters including supervising the withdrawal of foreign forces as well as demilitarisation. On the military side alone, it is estimated that the UN presence will run close to some 15,000 personnel.

There is, however, a major problem with all these peacekeeping and related activities. They are means of picking up the pieces once a conflict has concluded, a conflict that the UN could neither deter nor counter. The ability to stand between combatants who have agreed to stop fighting does not deter potential aggressors, and does not amount to the ability to stop wars once they have started. Peacemaking activities in the traditional sense (i.e. diplomacy), which sometimes do help bring about the end of a conflict, do not have that effect either. Yet, this is precisely what the United Nations was created to do.

Peacemaking as Peace Enforcement

I now come to a second and completely different meaning of peacemaking, best exemplified recently by Europeans in the context of the Yugoslav crisis, in order to distinguish their potential involvement in *peacekeeping*, i.e, an operation with the consent of all the parties, from the possibility of an *enforced* presence.

If this option was ultimately rejected by the Europeans in the case of Yugoslavia, it was adopted by the UN in the case of Iraq's invasion of Kuwait, under the name of "peace enforcement measures", to use the vocabulary of the UN Charter. It should be understood, however, that the Gulf Crisis was very different from any other situation. The United Nations Security Council was able to act in a manner closer than ever before to the objectives envisaged by the founders of the UN, in reacting speedily and effectively to an actual act of aggression *as it occurred*, under Chapter VII of the Charter, and not simply in devising peace-making and peacekeeping mechanisms *after the fact*. The reasons for this are several: *First*, the Iraqi invasion of Kuwait was a clear-cut case of aggression; *Second*, none of the major powers were involved or, at that point, considered Iraq to be a client state; *Third*, in a post Cold War context, the USA and the USSR and, more generally, the permanent members of the Council were prepared to work together with a view to ensuring international stability; *Fourth*, the views of the non-aligned states had evolved considerably — their automatic, sometimes ill-advised solidarity has broken down and they no longer formed a bloc irrevocably committed to one side or another; *Fifth*, the interests at stake were important enough to justify the injection of the massive resources required for the handling of the crisis.

The decision to initiate the eviction of Iraq from Kuwait by the use of force was, of course, a most difficult decision. But it was and remains the right one. After twelve Security Council resolutions — clear and unequivocal — imagine the implications of saying that, after all, the international community was just bluffing. What message would this give to future aggressors? And to states like Kuwait, which are not great powers?

Failure to act in such clear circumstances would have meant that the UN would be ignored in the future by major powers and potential aggressors alike. As the Canadian Prime Minister said in February of last year, a discredited UN would clearly make the world an even more dangerous place than it is already. Conversely, the success of this operation should not only discourage aggression: It should show to the military powers that there is no force more compelling than global consensus and unity. It should also demonstrate to all countries that the United Nations works as was intended, and can be relied upon to meet the challenges of the next century.

The handling of the Gulf Crisis by the UN has, of course, raised many legitimate questions. Some of them relate to the timing and impact of sanctions. To some extent, the debate continues today, as the persistent and, to most of us, incomprehensible tolerance demonstrated by Saddam Hussein for the suffering of his own people has so far prevented Iraq from taking advantage of the possibility formally offered to it by the Security Council to export oil with a view to providing humanitarian relief to the country.

Other questions relate to the conduct of collective action itself. Indeed, the Council was unable to use some of the mechanisms provided for it in Chapter VII of the UN Charter. First, under the Charter, states were supposed to make available to the Council, on call, armed forces, assistance and facilities. National Air Force contingents were to be made immediately available for combined enforcement action. Second, a military staff committee was to advise and assist the Council on military requirements as well as on the employment and command of armed forces. It would also be responsible under the Council for the strategic direction of armed forces placed at its disposal.

Neither mechanism was used in the Gulf Crisis. As the Cold War had prevented the establishment of "armed forces, assistance and facilities" at the disposition of the Council, the use of national armed forces of certain states was necessary. As for the military staff committee, it was alluded to in one of the resolutions of the Security Council, but was not, in fact, a player in the crisis and had no contact with members of the coalition. The Council itself did not make any "plans for the application of armed forces" as envisaged in Article 46 of the Charter.

Therefore, in the end, the multi-national operation in the Gulf was *not a UN force*, but rather a non-UN force operating under the authority of UN Security Council Resolution Number 678 which specifically authorized "member states cooperating with the government of Kuwait. . .to use all necessary means to uphold (the relevant) resolutions (of the Council) and to restore international peace and security in the area." This was in full conformity with the UN Charter which provides, in its Article 48, that the Security Council can designate some member states to carry out its decisions for the maintenance of international peace and security.

After the outbreak of hostilities, the Security Council met a few times in exceptional formal but closed meetings. On those occasions some member states expressed concerns over certain issues relating to the use of force against Iraq and the tenor of Resolution 678 itself. Generally speaking, these concerns focused on the fact that the Security Council did not actually control the conduct of hostilities. The authorization given in Resolution 678 was not limited in duration and did not define the kind of action or force that might be used to compel Iraqi withdrawal from Kuwait. The resolution required reporting from participating states, but there was no further guidance on the part of the Council. Suggestions were made that the objectives of the countries participating in the coalition might go beyond the intent of Resolution 678. The countries of the coalition, on the other hand, consistently maintained that their objectives remained those defined in the relevant resolutions, broad as they might have been, and they reported to the Council on the conduct of hostilities.

To sum up, the main effect of the Security Council's action in the Gulf Crisis has certainly been to increase the confidence of the international community in the will and capability of the United Nations to deal effectively with aggression. As I said earlier, some specific conditions have to be present for enforcement action to be taken, including a general disposition to cooperate among major powers. Yet, at a minimum, these events should give pause to potential aggressors, who now know there is a possibility that the UN will act against them — a possibility no one took seriously before this crisis. This operation has also raised some other important issues which will no doubt be widely debated in the months and years to come: The relative effect of sanctions and how much time should be given for them to be effective; the degree of direct control the Security Council should or should not have over an enforcement operation; the adequacy of the mechanisms that are now at the disposal of the Council, etc. Despite such questions, when you look back at the way the UN handled this crisis, it can only be seen as a remarkable achievement — a demonstration of unprecedented unity of vision and resolve which has not ended with the termination of hostilities but has been sustained to meet the difficult challenges of the post-hostilities period.

I refer here, of course, to the overwhelming approval by members of the Security Council of Resolution 687, one of the most complex and detailed UN Resolutions ever adopted. In setting out the terms and conditions for the implementation of a formal ceasefire, in *compelling* Iraq to neutralize and destroy its chemical, biological and nuclear weapons and its ballistic missiles over a certain range, to restrict future arms purchases, to accept the inviolability of Kuwait's frontiers, to pay reparations and renounce terrorism, the UN has demonstrated convincingly its ability not only to effectively *make* the peace but, equally important, its ability to *keep* the peace. This goes beyond its decision to deploy UN peacekeeping forces. By compelling Iraq to reduce military expenditures, the Security Council peace terms implicitly render any government in Baghdad less of a threat to its neighbours or its own people. By linking the removal of remaining sanctions to Iraqi compliance with the provisions of the resolution, the UN encourages the re-entry into the international community of a responsible Iraq. Several resolutions have been adopted since then, many of which also relate to Iraq's conduct on its own territory.

Peacemaking Within States

This leads me to a third meaning of "peacemaking" which is easy to understand in principle but more difficult to link to the United Nations we have traditionally known and is, in that context, conceptually revolutionary: the making of peace within the borders of a single state. From a humanitarian point of view, why should conflict, losses of lives and destruction be tolerated simply because no more than one state is involved? Why would the international community, which deploys so many efforts in resolving international conflicts, be inactive and even silent where the same tragedies occur within the borders of one sovereign state?

The answer has traditionally been disarmingly simple. In principle, the United Nations is prohibited by its own constitution, the Charter, from intervening in the internal affairs of its member states. And, if this is not enough, the mandate of the Security Council — the only organ that has the capacity for effective action in real terms — is restricted to issues affecting *international* peace and security.

This answer is not without validity, but it has always left some fundamental questions unanswered. In addition, the world has changed. Many issues that were traditionally considered essentially internal are now seen as being of legitimate international concern. This is true for problems which clearly cannot be resolved without international cooperation: How can you resolve most environmental or economic problems, for example, without thinking and acting on global issues? Also, the international *conscience* has changed. Many violations of human rights, for example, which were routinely ignored not so long ago, are now denounced and investigated much more promptly. I cannot imagine that large-scale tragedies such as those that occurred in Uganda or Cambodia a few years ago, could possibly be left off the agenda of the United Nations today for very long, as they were at the time.

Getting back to the narrower issue of peacemaking, the UN has of course contributed several times to the resolution of what are in essence internal conflicts, but always with a special reason justifying its action. In addition to classical decolonization issues such as Namibia and Western Sahara, the UN has played a very important role in helping re-establish peace among opposing factions in Nicaragua. It is now in the process of doing the same thing in El Salvador, and is expected to play an important political role in Angola and Cambodia. But this involvement can be explained in each case on the ground that these internal conflicts were by-products of regional conflicts threatening peace and security, thereby justifying a UN presence.

Iraq can also be described as a special case. Here, the UN's presence has been extraordinarily intrusive. First, and despite the convoluted way the issue was handled, the UN has provided a degree of protection, in effect, to Kurdish and Shiite minorities which were threatened by their own government on its own territory. Second, the UN has imposed a rigorous system, including

UN presence and freedom of action on Iraqi territory with a view to prohibiting the possession, production, acquisition by Iraq of certain types of weapons. Third, the UN continues to control — to a large extent, prevent — Iraq's external economic relations and trade, in order to force it to meet UN requirements for compensation to Kuwait and other states, financing of various UN operations and humanitarian assistance to its own population. But all this, again, can be justified through *ad hoc* reasons: We are, after all, in the process of ensuring that a declared aggressor is never again in a position to attack anyone else.

Since then, two other cases have come up: First, that of Yugoslavia, which was, at least in its origin, primarily an internal conflict but which had implications of going beyond Yugoslav borders. The Security Council was seized of the issue early on (by Canada, among a few others) and adopted a resolution imposing an arms embargo. In many ways, the conflict in Yugoslavia crystallizes well the preoccupation of some members states with UN participation in what is generally recognized to be an internal conflict — a civil war. With regard to Yugoslavia, the UN has taken a pragmatic approach which recognizes the effective absence of a central government and therefore, as a minimum, the need for the cooperation and consent of the parties to the conflict — Serbia, Croatia and the Yugoslavian National Army — before it elaborates on the details of a peacekeeping operation based upon the traditional criteria, not the least of which is an effective ceasefire.

Then came the overthrow of the democratically elected government of President Aristide in Haiti. Despite UN involvement in supervising that election, recent developments were clearly internal with little or no connection to international peace and security. In this case, the Security Council did not adopt a resolution. But it met, for the first time ever, on a purely internal issue, and it authorized its President to make a statement declaring this situation unacceptable. In the meantime, the Organization of American States, an organization which is also prohibited from intervening in internal affairs of its members, announced sanctions against Haiti.

So, something is changing. But can the United Nations do even more? Can it be expected to intervene physically on the territory of states where a civil war rages? or where human rights are violated on a massive scale? or where humanitarian assistance is denied by a government to starving populations?

This question cannot be definitively answered today. As I mentioned earlier, the UN is not a supranational government. It can only do what its members allow it to do. This action cannot be out-of-sync, so to speak, with the psychology of states. I doubt that the type of physical intervention I was mentioning would be accepted by most states as we speak today, and not only because of a few profoundly anti-democratic states — the Chinas, Cubas and Viet Nams of this world. More generally, intervention in internal affairs raises concern because, in this very century, it has been much abused. There is nothing easier for a powerful state than to disguise a desire to conquer, or to dominate, behind humanitarian concerns. So, weaker states are very wary about the tendency of stronger states — which are often without the kind of internal problems that so many developing states encounter — to favour an expansion in the number of cases in which intervention should be considered permissible.

Having said that, the final chapter of this story has not been written. The world is changing too fast for words. Developments in Eastern Europe and in the former Soviet Union, for example, have created an unprecedented situation, to which no known terms of reference apply. It may well be that the psychology of states will have changed so much in a not so distant future, that the UN will indeed be able to make peace not only among states, but also within them.

Before concluding, I wish to say a word on an important weak link in the UN system which needs our attention. From Canada's perspective, recent events have highlighted once again, and more vividly than ever, an issue that has long been a concern of ours: effective United Nations enforcement, or the lack of an effective UN role in the *prevention* of conflicts. It is encouraging to note that states have paid much more attention to this issue in the past few years. The General Assembly adopted a declaration on the prevention of conflicts in 1988, and last year endorsed a declaration on a fact-finding role for the organization. Nevertheless, despite the concern for this issue expressed by the former Secretary-General in his last three annual reports, this interest has yet to translate into appropriate mechanisms and concrete action. It is a difficult subject, which raises a number of practical and political problems, but it is an important one and it has to be dealt with. I believe that the success of the United Nations in the area of peace and security can only be complete when it has shown it is able not only to *remove* threats to peace, but also to *prevent* them, as provided in the very first paragraph of Article 1 of the Charter.

Imperfections there are but, even though some old differences remain and new divisions may appear, the international community is unlikely to return to the kind of fundamental tensions and opposition that existed a few years ago. Most states now seem genuinely interested in maintaining a degree of stability and cooperation in international relations. If this is true, the Security Council of the UN remains a tool that offers unique opportunities and a great deal of flexibility. At the United Nations, where there is a political will there is a practical way. In the final analysis, the Security Council is a mirror of the international community which can and will be effective if that is what states want. Indications are that most states now are much more interested in peace than ever before.

Questions & Answers

Q. Colonel Murray C. Johnston, Conference of Defence Associations

At the Citizen's Inquiry into Peace and Security last October some representatives of peace groups presented some contrasting positions. On the one hand they wanted the Armed Forces to be drastically reduced, while on the other they wanted increased resources available for peacekeeping. And they were also concerned that Canada should show a "peace dividend". Of course I and others reminded the panel that defence expenditures over the years had been very small and were becoming smaller in relation to the total government budget. Therefore the peace dividend would be non-existent. On the matter of Iraq, these people had shown sympathy towards Saddam Hussein which was entirely misplaced. In 1945 the German's complied with the terms of the surrender. But in 1991-92 Iraq was not complying with the United Nations terms, and hence the UN sanctions are still in place. Saddam is holding the world hostage to the extent he can. Could you comment on Canada's participation in peacekeeping and the cost implications?

A. The UN has a broader task now and the cost may rise to as much as 2 billion dollars, at a guess.

Q. John Toogood, Canadian Institute for International Peace and Security

My question is about Yugoslavia. The CSCE, the European Community and then the United Nations have all attempted to create peace in Yugoslavia. When the UN came along it fared better than the other two. Why is that?

A. The United Nations Charter tells us that the political solutions are to be tried first. Lord Carrington did not have the full support of the EC when he attempted to mediate the fighting, and the various factions in Yugoslavia were well aware of that. Therefore the EC failed in its effort. Cyrus Vance, on the other hand, had the full support of the Security Council.

Q. Colonel Butson, Defence Medical Association

My question is about the Antarctic. This is a very sensitive region. What if an oil company were to establish itself there with nuclear equipment and wanted to settle a community there?

A. The activity in the Antarctic is United Nations driven, and as the area is an internationally-agreed nuclear weapons-free-zone, this scenario is very unlikely.

Q. Vice Admiral J. Anderson, Maritime Command

What do you think of the suggestion to have a peacekeeping training centre located in Nova Scotia?

A. There is a peacekeeping committee at the United Nations, and now many new countries are contributing to peacekeeping operations. For example, there are operations in the Spanish-speaking countries and we therefore have need for Spanish-speaking peacekeepers. We have been asked to assist the UN in developing expertise in a variety of types of expertise useful to peacekeeping.

Q. (Director of Logistics Operations)

Considering that the USSR is disintegrating and in decline, and considering also the status of the British and French memberships in the United Nations, what is your prognosis for the Security Council?

A. Germany and Japan are not represented, are not part of the Security Council; it no longer reflects the worlds geo-political realities. The Security Council needs change. This is unlikely to happen very soon but will happen eventually.

Editor's Note:

Some difficulty was experienced with the recording facility, so this question period has been reconstructed as well as human memory permits.

VII

Canadian Defence Policy and the International Strategic Environment

by
The Honourable Marcel Masse, P.C., M.P.
Minister of National Defence

I wish this morning to discuss with you three subjects that are of keen interest to us all, and concerning which I know you still have a number of questions.

I shall begin with an overview of the highlights of the defence policy that I announced on September 17th. I will then say a few words about the financial considerations that affected the parameters of the new policy. And finally, I will place the policy in the global strategic context that shaped its major components.

Significance of Defence Associations in Canada

But first, allow me to tell you just how much I value the member-associations of the Conference of Defence Associations, and how much I appreciate their work and their energy.

In a democratic society, it has always been essential that issues of national importance be publicly discussed and debated. Only in this way can citizens make sound choices. Seen from this standpoint, the CDA plays an important role in stimulating discussion and increasing public understanding of defence. I commend your efforts, and I thank you.

Since 1932, relations between your organization and the Department have been friendly and constructive, although not without a few wrinkles. If filmmaker Emile de Antonio was right in 1967 when he said "the only way democracy can function is to have a diversity of opinion," then your organization has played an eminently democratic role, beginning with the 1932 debate on the reorganization of the Militia right up to the current debates on our defence policy.

From its origins as a simple lobby group whose purpose was to improve the welfare of its members, the CDA soon became involved in broader issues concerning the role of the Armed Forces, global security and defence policy. The establishment in 1966 of a "Thinkers' Seminar," and in January 1991 of a Defence Policy Committee, clearly illustrates the broader role that has evolved over the years. I see this role as a valuable contribution to democracy, and as part of a debate that is essential to our society.

New Policy Overview

On September 17th, 1991, I set forth a new defence policy. The policy statement basically described how our Armed Forces would fulfil Canada's traditional commitment to contribute to international peace and stability in a radically changed and still uncertain global environment.

The policy therefore stems less from changes in our overall purpose than from a profound alteration in the conditions surrounding them. Hence:

— Canada will continue to search for collective security through the United Nations and collective defence through NATO and through our continental defence relationship with the United States;

— The new policy also recognizes the disappearance of the specific Soviet threat, but reaffirms the need for effective and versatile forces capable of defending our interests at home and abroad.

The priorities for our forces are:

— First, defence, sovereignty and civil responsibilities in Canada;

— Second, collective defence arrangements through NATO, including our continental defence partnership with the United States; and

— Third, international peace and security through stability and peacekeeping operations, arms control verification and humanitarian assistance.

I also announced a related series of measures:

Canada will be reducing its military presence in Europe. By 1995, we will have reduced our forces stationed in Europe to a task force of some eleven hundred military personnel. We will close our two bases in Germany and return the CF-18s located in Baden-Soellingen to Canada.

We will nevertheless continue to ensure that we can respond to international crises. Specifically, Canada will maintain the capability to deploy a contingency brigade group and two operational CF-18 squadrons abroad.

I believe our most important task in implementing this policy is that of equipping our forces. As I said in September, "The Canadian Forces have earned an outstanding reputation for discipline, effectiveness and professionalism. It is incumbent upon us to provide them with equipment commensurate with their proficiency. That is one of the most important objectives of our policy."

To be able to do so, however, the budgetary constraints that I will describe in a few moments require the Department to reduce the amount it currently spends on personnel and infrastructure. With this in mind, I announced a reduction in the size of the Regular Force — from eighty-four thousand to seventy-six thousand by 1995 — and in the Department's complement of civilian personnel — from thirty-three thousand to thirty-two thousand over the same period.

I have also set up a working group which will report back to me in the spring on potential steps the Department could take to rationalize its existing infrastructure.

That, very briefly, is an overview of the new defence policy.

The Financial Squeeze: a Western Problem

I will move on shortly to the assessment of the international environment which shaped our new policy. I must emphasize, however, that the strategic concept that underpins sound policy cannot be comprised of international factors alone. Without due regard to domestic conditions, any new defence policy and programs would be doomed to failure. That is why we began our review by examining the domestic factors that limit what we *can* do, and then proceeded to design our programs accordingly.

In Canada, as in other industrialized countries at this time, the first limitation on any new policy is a financial one. It is certainly false to claim that the availability of funds *determines* the nature of defence policy. It is more accurate to say that budgetary imperatives force policy-makers to make more difficult choices on how to implement the policy.

In this sense, the Department of National Defence has had to submit for several years to the same exercise as all other government departments — that is, of adjusting its plans in light of the Government's overriding priority of deficit reduction. Being realistic about this is the only way for policy-makers to avoid failure — and to ensure that the policy uses our available resources to their greatest effect.

The whole issue is, therefore, to determine how to rationalize our operations in order to realize savings and apply our resources to our aims in the most effective manner. Mission impossible? Certainly not! A challenge to our collective intellect and imagination? Definitely — and I am proud of the Department, which has accomplished this task brilliantly.

The International Context: the Need for a Flexible Strategy

What can we say about the international context, which is one of the fundamental and, by definition, *permanent*, parameters of our policy?

To begin with, it is important to remember that Canada is a middle power whose world role is conditioned by the prevailing structure of international relations. This structure, in turn, shapes the specific roles we play within our alliance relationships. To say the least, these relations are currently undergoing fundamental change. It is therefore not at all surprising that our new policy should tend towards being flexible and pragmatic rather than inflexible and doctrinaire.

The end of the Cold War is unquestionably the most important development in international relations since 1945. For nearly half a century, we have become accustomed to thinking and analyzing in terms of two antagonistic blocs. All our policies were, implicitly or explicitly, conditioned by this antagonism. Now it no longer exists, and international relations are in a state of flux. The rigid structures of the bipolar world have been replaced by new political alignments — sometimes, one might add, only to make way for emerging nationalism, territorial conflict and ethnic disputes. We are not sure where it will all lead.

Europe

Our analysis of the international environment begins with Europe. Europe, the front line of the Cold War, also represented the boundary between two views of the world. On one side of this boundary was an alliance of free and democratic states which, under the umbrella of NATO and the European Community, enjoyed prosperity and security. On the other side was the Warsaw Pact, where nations were forced to subscribe to the leaden ideology of Marxism-Leninism.

The final bankruptcy of this ideology was inevitable. By the mid-80s, the lamentable state of the Soviet economy was clear. We know the rest. Gorbachev took power and introduced Glasnost and Perestroika — openness and restructuring. The Soviet Union abandoned the Brezhnev Doctrine. These factors were soon to lead to democratic revolution in Eastern Europe, the dismantlement of the Berlin wall, the unification of Germany, and the collapse of the Warsaw Pact. At the same time, the Soviet Union became much more cooperative in a variety of arms control fora. In rethinking its own military stance, the USSR accepted the principle of transparency set out in the Stockholm Declaration, and of asymmetrical reductions in the Treaty on Intermediate-Range Nuclear Forces; agreed to on-site verification; and even began unilateral troop withdrawals.

Western nations responded to these developments with prudence. Moreover, we have urged the reformers to strive for greater liberalism at home and greater cooperation abroad.

The end of the Cold War is certainly something to be celebrated. But we also recognize that the changes in Central Europe, combined with the crumbling of the former Soviet Union, have led to a host of new problems. These problems call for a redefinition of our security situation — and of the contribution military forces can make in resolving them.

It is obvious, for example, that the new democracies are all the more fragile for their serious economic problems, ethnic tensions and rapid movements of refugees. Under such conditions, the support of the people for the new regimes could erode and bring non-democratic tendencies to the fore.

Clearly, too, the break-up of the USSR has set in motion forces rife with the potential for violent conflict. Certainly, we and our allies are very concerned about what will happen to the Soviet military apparatus. We have identified as one of our priorities the ratification and implementation of agreements in the Strategic Arms Reduction Talks and in the negotiations on Conventional Forces in Europe. Achieving these goals remains important to building a stable world order and true international cooperation.

Seen from this standpoint, the establishment of democratic governments in Central and Eastern Europe calls for certain initiatives on our part. This is why Canada, among other things, helped create the North Atlantic Cooperation Council. This institution is designed to promote dialogue between NATO and former Warsaw Pact countries.

As far as the Canadian Forces are concerned, I would envisage *three* roles for our military personnel in the new European order.

First, *collective security and defence*. This principle provides the continuing rationale for NATO. At their Summit in Rome last November, Alliance heads of state and government reaffirmed the intrinsic value of collective defence.

Second, with respect to our involvement in *peacekeeping forces and observer missions*, the instability and ethnic conflict in Europe could require the intervention of multinational peacekeeping forces. As an example, we have just sent a team of observers to Yugoslavia.

Finally, CF personnel will continue to be involved in *arms control and verification activities* — with respect not only to the implementation of the treaty on Conventional Forces in Europe, but to the negotiation and implementation of new initiatives as well. Our service personnel will also be called upon to enhance and preserve the general climate of trust and openness through meetings and discussions at the staff level.

Canadian defence policy is attuned to the new security environment. We have witnessed the end of the Cold War and the establishment of a more equal and stable balance of forces. It was on this basis that the Government of Canada took the decision to reduce our military presence in Europe. But we will remain active in European security affairs. Currently under discussion with our allies and with NATO military authorities are the role and location of the stationed task force of eleven hundred personnel. This formation meets NATO's requirement to have forces that are more mobile and flexible. Furthermore, our other NATO commitments will remain unchanged. These include our NATO naval commitments; our participation in the Allied Command Europe Mobile Force (Land) and in the NATO Composite Force; and our contribution to NATO commonly-funded programs.

North America

We have used the same approach — of modifying our policy to fit the new circumstances — when assessing our North American defence requirements.

As the century draws to a close, we must recognize that threats to a country's sovereignty do not stem solely from military action. A nation must also be able to enforce its own laws with those who would pollute its environment, fish illegally in its waters, or use its air or maritime approaches for illegal drug trafficking. With the end of the East-West confrontation which, in the past, determined the general thrust of our military activity, we can now assign even greater importance to these problems.

Our current policy maintains all of our bilateral agreements with the United States, including the renewed NORAD Agreement. While it is clear that the strategic context of North American defence is in transition, most of our continental air defence capability will be required in any strategic context.

The Developing World

Lastly, our analysis led us to the conclusion that regional conflicts will persist in certain other parts of the world, fuelled by such problems as demographic pressure, ethnic tensions, and desperate economic conditions. Such conflicts could be exacerbated by the proliferation of advanced weaponry in the developing world. This is why we are working to control the transfer of arms.

Iraq's invasion of Kuwait illustrated how international relations can suddenly turn for the worse — and how a prompt response by the international community can restore the rule of law. That is why Canada will maintain, for example, the capacity to deploy two squadrons of CF-18s and an expeditionary force anywhere in the world and at any time.

By contrast, we are also seeing more settlements obtained by negotiations under the aegis of the United Nations. In Central America and Cambodia, for example, international efforts of this kind are being accepted by belligerents in areas that would, in the past, have been considered as strictly internal matters — such as the monitoring of elections.

Canada will continue to consider any new requests for peace-keeping assistance. The new policy provides for the maintenance of standby forces to participate in multilateral peacekeeping and observer missions. Normally, these will consist of a battle group, along with the associated communications and air transport support elements.

All these roles — collective security and defence, peacekeeping, humanitarian missions and assistance to civil authorities — essentially require forces that are well equipped and, above all, flexible. The new defence policy's emphasis on the maintenance of flexible, capable forces will leave us well-placed to respond to the varying needs of the international community.

Conclusion

I shall conclude this brief overview with two comments.

First, as I trust I've been able to show here today, our new policy is based on a global analysis of the international situation in which change appears to be the only constant feature.

The challenge for all of us is to change a mind-set that has developed over almost fifty years, in order to be able to understand the situation as a *whole*. And although the old situation no longer exists, our task is complicated by the continuing state of flux in the new one.

Second, it is also important to explain to Canadians the whys and wherefores of our defence policy. The Cold War was clear-cut and easy to understand. Things are no longer so. The current international situation is fragmented, constantly changing and unpredictable. The dangers may be smaller, but they are infinitely more numerous.

Let me conclude by offering you this assurance: the Canadian Forces *will* have the means to implement the defence policy I announced in September. They will be leaner, to be sure, but they will be better equipped and able to carry out all their missions with the skill and professionalism for which they are known.

VIII

1991 in Review

by
General A.J.G.D. de Chastelain
Chief of the Defence Staff

As the Minister described in his speech earlier this morning, the international strategic environment in which the Canadian Forces operate changed during 1991 with a speed and significance that none among us could have imagined beforehand. The year began dramatically with Canadian troops joined in a multinational effort to force Iraqi troops from Kuwait. And with equal drama, the year closed on the Soviet Union disintegrating amid political revolution. International strife characterized 1991, but so did the quest for peace and security. Canadian troops stood duty as peacekeepers on four continents and their participation in NATO and NORAD made a valued contribution to our collective defence.

My main purpose this morning is to review with you the diverse activities conducted by the Canadian Forces during 1991 — activities that included combat, peacekeeping, arms verification, humanitarian relief and search and rescue operations. I will start with a quick tour d'horizon of world activities. Then, I will specifically examine a series of issues including: CF activities in the international security environment; the Forces' response to domestic imperatives; DND's adjustment to budgetary restraint; equipment acquisitions; and the military response to social change. Finally, I will turn my attention to the new defence policy and its impact on the CF.

As illustrated by the Gulf Crisis, the upheaval in the former Soviet Union, and the civil war in Yugoslavia — to name just three — the Canadian Forces must prepare for an increasingly unpredictable future. Unfortunately, there is every prospect that the international strife witnessed in 1991 will continue — a situation that I believe underscores the need to field mobile, combat-capable armed forces with a general-purpose ability.

As a consequence of this less Europe-centered threat, the defence policy announced last September has already led to a shift in the focus of Canadian military activity. The basic principles of security under which the Canadian Forces operate have not changed. But the emphasis once placed on countering the Soviet threat against North America, the North Atlantic and Central Europe has been redirected to providing versatile general-purpose forces for the defence of Canadian interests anywhere.

CF Response to the New International Security Environment

It is in the context of a fast-changing and explosive world that the CF operated in 1991. During the Gulf Crisis our forces played a meaningful and effective part in the multinational coalition that assembled to enforce the United Nations' sanctions against Iraq. By the end of the war, more than thirty-three hundred CF Regulars and Reservists, close to seven percent of them women, had participated.

Canada's naval contribution to the Coalition included the provision of a naval task group and the coordination and control of the logistic support at sea for the more than 120 Coalition ships in the Gulf.

Also carrying out operations in the Gulf were a squadron of CF-18 fighters, headquarters, logistic and air support personnel, a signals squadron, two infantry security companies, a field hospital, a medical unit that served aboard a US hospital ship and an air-to-air refuelling tanker. Each of the units dispatched to the Gulf achieved unqualified success in their operations and earned the respect of their allied counterparts.

We will be studying the lessons learned from the Gulf War for some time. Three of them deserve special mention now. First, Gulf operations proved the value of maintaining forces capable of adjusting quickly and easily to contingencies. Second, the Coalition's forces demonstrated the benefits of the military cooperation routinely exercised in collective defence organizations such as NATO and NORAD. The third lesson is the utility of being supported by bases close to the scene of action. For future operations, we are going to have to plan ahead to establish intermediary theatre bases.

We took another step towards cooperation and security in May, when the Soviet Chief of the General Staff visited Canada for the first time. General Moiseyev's visit was significant for an additional reason. In an effort to build mutual confidence and promote security, we signed an agreement aimed at the prevention of dangerous military activities. Although we have witnessed the break-up of the Soviet Union, we expect the Soviet successor republics to abide by this document, which will reduce the potential for incidents when armed forces of Canada and the republics exercise or operate in close proximity.

The spirit of cooperation continued in September when a team from Canadian Forces Base Lahr conducted Canada's first challenge inspection of a military exercise in the former Soviet Union. As the inspection illustrated, the Canadian Forces have taken an active role in promoting "transparency" in arms control and military relations.

The team observed activities in the Leningrad Military District and verified that none of them were contrary to the provisions of the Vienna Document. You may recall that in 1990 Canada signed the Vienna Document, an agreement which aims to enhance confidence as European security relations move from confrontation to co-operation.

Canada further demonstrated its commitment to arms control in November by ratifying the Treaty on Conventional Forces in Europe, an agreement that requires signing parties to reduce stocks of military equipment. Under the terms of the Treaty, CF verification teams immediately scheduled on-site inspections in Eastern Europe and what was then the Soviet Union.

Our contribution to international security through peacekeeping also continued apace in 1991. Late in the year, Canada sent 11 observers to the European Community Multinational Monitoring Mission in Yugoslavia. We also recently joined, for the first time, UNAVEM in Angola — a mission originally created in 1989. Canadian forces have now served in all of the UN peacekeeping operations, including 5 new ones created last year. At year's end more than 1,000 CF members, including 100 Reservists and almost 60 women, were contributing to 13 separate peacekeeping operations.

Between May and October three hundred Canadian field engineers of 3 CER undertook the difficult and dangerous task of clearing mines and explosives and patrolling the buffer zone between Iraq and Kuwait. Eighty-five Canadian servicemen and women of 5 RGC are continuing the task.

As participants in a UN special commission, CF members also inspected chemical, nuclear and biological facilities and ballistic missile sites in Iraq. Both CF and DND personnel are still serving on the commission.

While the deployment of more than seven hundred soldiers from the Canadian Airborne Regiment to the Western Sahara has been delayed, the advance party, including the mission's military force commander, Major-General Armand Roy, was in place by year's end. MINURSO, as the mission is called, is monitoring a ceasefire established last fall and its mandate is to oversee a referendum later this year.

In August, a Reserve officer arrived in El Salvador where a UN mission will monitor the recently-signed agreement between the government and the Farabundo Marti National Liberation Front. At the end of this month, twenty-four CF officers will be transferred to El Salvador from another Central American mission to serve in this monitoring process.

An additional 30 CF officers will assist in monitoring the initial peace period following the El Salvador ceasefire. Recently, we agreed to provide up to five more officers for this mission, if requested by the UN.

Last September in Angola, fifteen CF personnel joined the UN mission whose mandate had been to assist in the withdrawal of Cuban troops. That mission is now monitoring a ceasefire between government and rebel forces in anticipation of an election planned for this September.

Finally, in 1991, two CF officers brought their expertise to the advance mission tasked with monitoring a ceasefire in Cambodia's longstanding civil war. The mandate of the Cambodian mission, which is also establishing a mine awareness program, may be expanded in future.

To bring you up to date on Canada's contribution to international stability, let me mention Yugoslavia. Canada has eleven CF members monitoring and observing the ceasefire with other EC observers,all of them under the auspices of the Conference on Security and Cooperation in Europe. In addition, three CF members are part of fifty military observers who have recently been dispatched in the latest UN initiative to resolve that civil war.

The Forces' ability and readiness to respond to international calls for humanitarian aid was tested three times last year. Between April and June, a CF medical team largely drawn from CFE, aided Kurdish and Iraqi refugees massed along the Turkish border.

As part of the same relief effort, a Boeing and two C130s ferried emergency supplies to refugees in Iraq, Turkey and Iran. In Ethiopia, C130 aircraft airlifted sixteen thousand tonnes of relief supplies throughout the country on behalf of the UN World Food Program. And finally, two Boeing flights airlifted Red Cross supplies to Yugoslavia in December.

Earlier this month, in NATO's first-ever humanitarian mission, a CF Boeing flew fifty-four tonnes of milk powder into Moscow to meet some of the basic needs of the Russian people.

CF Response to Domestic Imperatives

In carrying out their domestic roles, the Forces also faced challenges in 1991. Prominent among activities at home were search and rescue operations and sovereignty protection.

Fortunately, our Forces were not called out in Aid of the Civil Power as they were the year before. But I am hopeful that the dialogue we established with the provincial civil authorities during the Oka Crisis will foster public understanding of our role, in Aid of the Civil Power.

A discussion of search and rescue activities brings to mind the tragic Hercules crash in the Arctic last October. The rescue of survivors was accomplished through the extraordinary effort of the SAR technicians who jumped into the crash site, of the CF personnel who fought their way overland to the site and of the survivors themselves. The remote location, the harsh weather and the hazardous terrain conspired to make this rescue attempt extremely difficult. The fact that they were successful is a testimony to the determination of all who were involved.

As you know, CF search and rescue resources are on alert twenty-four hours every day. SAR units are equipped and trained to respond to air and maritime distress incidents *anywhere* in Canada, although well over 90 percent of sea rescues and over 90 percent of air rescues take place south of 60. Included in the Canadian Forces SAR capability is a contingency plan (MAJAID), to provide resources in response to a major air disaster in the North.

Additional points include:

a. The Canadian Forces operate the space-based distress alert system known as SARSAT in addition to the command and control system that coordinates the activities of SAR squadrons across Canada.

b. We constantly review our SAR capabilities and initiate improvements to equipment and procedures. Two examples:

(1) The MAJAID Plan is in the final stages of a two-year revision process. Originally, disaster kits able to support 80 personnel were located only at CFB Edmonton. These have been redistributed with half the kits now at CFB Trenton and half remaining at CFB Edmonton. This change will improve the flexibility of the response to an air disaster in the Arctic.

(2) The second example deals with the problem of recovering para-dropped survival equipment in strong winds. Frequently, the load cannot be recovered before the parachute drags the equipment away. To remedy this problem, a prototype device to release the equipment from its parachute on impact is being developed. It will undergo trials this year.

In addition, special SAR square parachutes, which we have been developing for a couple of years, will be delivered to SAR units beginning this summer. So will portable Global Positioning System navigation instruments.

As in past years, the Forces assisted the Department of Fisheries by dedicating ninety-five days to fisheries patrols on the Atlantic and Pacific coasts. Aurora aircraft flew additional surveillance on the East Coast, a role Arcturus aircraft will assume next year. Our ships and aircraft also assisted the RCMP with drug interdiction activities.

In 1991, Canada renewed its NORAD agreement with the U.S.A. for a further five-year period. NORAD remains an efficient, cost-effective means for maintaining Canadian national security and protecting our sovereignty through the provision of prompt and reliable information on incursions and threats to our airspace.

Although the risk of war between the superpowers has diminished, the republics of the former Soviet Union still possess enormous nuclear arsenals, and NORAD's early warning and attack assessment capability still underpin Canada's air and aerospace defence. As threats to security and stability shift with the changing times, NORAD resources can be directed to meeting additional priorities, such as drug interdiction.

The Military Adjustment to Budgetary Restraint

One of the major factors in the change in defence policy last year was the need to meet the budgetary constraints confronting Canadians. The requirement to reduce the accumulated national debt made further demands on DND's need to pursue an affordable policy — reshaping the defence program to fit the resources available.

A policy with less resources and fewer people means that while we will not compromise on effectiveness, we *will do less.* That fact translates into fewer or reduced operational capabilities.

Budget cuts announced in 1989 and 1990 led to the reorganization last year of air resources in Canada and Europe. Changes include:

— replacing Buffalo aircraft with Hercules to enhance our SAR capability on the East Coast;

— disbanding a fighter squadron in Germany and reassigning pilots and aircraft to other European-based squadrons, thereby maintaining NATO commitments;

— retiring the Chinook and disbanding one of the two CH-147 helicopter squadrons — a consequence of rationalizing resources — while re-equipping the other squadron with Twin Hueys and reorganizing it as a Total Force unit;

— replacing the Hercules with the Dash 8 for air navigation training;

— moving two squadrons — a search and rescue squadron from Summerside to Greenwood and a transport squadron from Winnipeg to Trenton; and

— announcing plans to divide and relocate the electronic warfare squadron from North Bay to Comox and Shearwater with expanded roles.

The army also had to make do with less in 1991 when our troops in Canadian Forces Europe were reduced by 1400.

When current reductions in personnel at National Defence Headquarters are completed, they should result in annual savings of forty million dollars. Based on the findings of the NDHQ Functional Review, about five hundred military and five hundred civilian positions will be eliminated during the implementation period. Sixty-five percent of the reductions were achieved during the fiscal year 1991-92. Affected CF members are being reassigned, while every attempt is being made to relocate the affected civilians within DND or other government departments. Over two hundred civilians have left the public service under the voluntary provisions of the Workforce Adjustment Program with associated benefits. More reductions are planned starting in 1993.

To meet fiscal realities, some equipment programs have been cancelled or reduced. Plans to purchase additional small arms and TOW under armour systems were cancelled. As well, ammunition stocks will be reduced over time, resulting in an estimated spending reduction of four hundred million dollars.

As another cost-effective measure, a contract for flight training was awarded to the private sector. Bombardier-Canadair will head the group that will train military student pilots for the next five years at a contract cost of one hundred and sixty-five million dollars.

New approaches to both training and operations were part of the continued development of the Total Force. The commitment to integrate the Reserve and Regular Forces moved ahead with the opening of Land Forces Western Area last summer. Two more areas in Quebec and the Maritimes are scheduled for opening this summer.

In June, Treasury Board approved the design phase of a new Naval Reserve facility at Pointe-à-Carcy, Quebec, which will house a fleet school, Naval Reserve Headquarters and the Naval Reserve Division NCSM Montcalm.

The establishment of this naval reserve facility was the third phase of the Naval Presence in Quebec Project. To briefly put this phase in context, I would remind everyone that phase one — in July 1983 — involved moving Naval Reserve Headquarters from Halifax to rented facilities in Quebec City. And phase two — during 1985-86 — saw three new Naval Reserve Divisions established in temporary quarters in Trois-Rivières, Chicoutimi and Rimouski.

Concurrent with the development of the Total Force, DND is improving compensation for Reservists. During 1991, a health

care program and a number of group insurance plans were
extended to Reservists.

New Equipment Programs

Despite fiscal difficulties, re-equipment remains a priority to
allow the Forces to keep abreast of developing technology.

During the year, major re-equipment initiatives included the
award of a 1.3 billion dollar contract to a consortium led by
Computing Devices for the delivery of the Iris mobile field radio
system beginning in 1994-95. Long-range communication capabilities will make the system effective even in the most remote
reaches of the Arctic.

On the East Coast, the first of the Canadian Patrol Frigates,
HMCS Halifax, was delivered to the navy. Eight of the twelve
frigates are in various stages of production, with four of the eight
afloat. Additionally, HMCS Algonquin, the first modernized Tribal
Class destroyer, was provisionally accepted. Two other Tribals
are in various stages of the modernization program and HMCS
Huron, the last ship of the class, will enter the program this spring.

On the West Coast, the construction of a ship repair unit and
jetty was completed at a cost of fifty million dollars. It will
accommodate warships well into the next century.

Plans to refit HMCS Protecteur, the supply ship that served
in the Gulf, were announced in October. Protecteur will begin
a refit next fall that will include permanent installation of a self-
defence system.

In CFB Petawawa, construction is underway on two sets of
singles quarters in anticipation of the arrival of the First Battalion,
The Royal Canadian Regiment from London, Ontario. A contract
will be let in March for a new junior ranks dining hall and the
contract for a transport and maintenance building is expected
to be tendered this spring. In addition, the move of 1 RCR has
accelerated our plans for the construction a new ammunition
storage facility. The first phase of this project should be tendered
this summer.

At our Militia Training and Support Centre in Meaford, we completed the final design of half the facilities and the preliminary design for the rest. This year, we will begin the construction of outside service roads and utilities.

The construction of the Militia Training and Support Centre in Valcartier has been accelerated. The field camp is expected to be completed in December 1994 with the remainder of the project completed in March 1997.

In Gagetown, major construction begun in 1990 for the Combat Training Centre Complex will be completed this year, with some final touches extending into 1993.

The army will also benefit from the contract signed with Western Star Trucks of Kelowna, B.C., for close to three thousand light trucks. The two hundred million dollar order will include troop transport, cargo and special use vehicles and will replace the current fleet built in the mid-seventies.

The CF and Social Change/Societal Demands

The military, like any other organization, is affected by the social trends and pressures that influence its workforce. To ensure that our personnel policies are based on a solid understanding of social issues, the National Defence Consultative Committee on Social Change was formed in November. Committee members are studying the factors that affect our policies and will recommend changes to allow us to make improvements while maintaining operational effectiveness.

The Associate Minister announced a program last year to promote family life and social well-being in the military community by providing a variety of services at bases and stations.

Environmental issues also received special attention. The Biological and Chemical Defence Review Committee's first annual report was released in August. It concluded that our biological and chemical defence programs are strictly defensive in character, are managed in a professional manner, and pose no threat to public safety or to the environment.

The New Defence Policy and Its Impact on the CF

Responding to the international and domestic factors I mentioned earlier, the government began a review of its defence policy in 1989, culminating with the Minister's announcement last September. As I have noted already, modifications to the policy represent a shift in focus to maintain flexible, general-purpose, combat-capable armed forces.

The three pillars of Canadian security policy — defence and collective security; arms control and disarmament; and the peaceful resolution of disputes — remain unchanged.

The Forces' three priorities are still clearly defined to be defence, sovereignty and civil responsibilities at home; collective defence through NATO and our continental partnership with the United States; and international peace and security through involvement in stability operations, peacekeeping, arms control verification and humanitarian assistance.

To afford new equipment, we must make economies, reducing expenditures on personnel, operations and maintenance. We will operate a leaner force.

With the changes to our personnel and infrastructure just mentioned by the Minister, we hope to save one half-billion dollars compared to the 1991 federal budget planning levels. But even with the substantial economies we have made, we will still require a small annual increase in the defence budget to maintain operations.

As costs in other areas are reduced over the next four years, the capital portion of the budget is expected to increase from the current 22 percent of defence spending to 26 percent. In the longer term, the aim is to increase capital expenditures to 30 percent.

The navy will continue to focus its attention on our East and West Coasts. Control over Canadian waters, including the detection and surveillance of submarines, will be exercised by a fleet of sixteen frigates and destroyers, the first four of a series of six corvettes, three of a planned six submarines and a dozen coastal defence vessels. A five hundred million dollar contract for the coastal defence vessels was let in October.

This fleet balance will enable us to broaden the scope of our maritime activities. We will possess a greater capacity to assist civil authorities with drug interdiction, fisheries patrols, resource protection and other activities. Efforts will also be made to achieve a better balance of naval capability between the East and West Coasts and to improve Arctic surveillance.

There will be no significant reduction in our Maritime Forces personnel, which number about ten thousand. Enrolment in both the Naval Reserve and the maritime element of the Supplementary Reserve will increase in keeping with the Total Force concept. The navy is well aware of the value of its Reserves. Seventeen naval reservists served in the Gulf — nine aboard warships.

A more mobile, flexible army — also based on Total Force — will maintain a general-purpose combat capability. As we integrate the army and the militia, the command structure will be reorganized along regional lines. In addition to the Task Force that will replace our current land commitment in Europe, we will continue to maintain the capability to deploy a battalion group as part of the ACE Mobile Force or the NATO Composite Force.

A brigade group will also be in readiness for contingency operations anywhere in the world; and a battalion group will continue to be equipped and trained to respond to UN peace-keeping requests abroad and to Aid of the Civil Power requirements at home.

For quick response, the army will be equipped with multi-role combat vehicles, heavy anti-tank weapons, modernized howitzers and the range of new small arms. The main battle tanks in Germany will remain in service for several more years, but will eventually be replaced by an Armoured Combat Vehicle (ACV) variant of the multi-role combat vehicle.

Aside from the return of CF-18 squadrons currently based in Germany, air force roles and activities will change little under the new policy. Emphasis will still be placed on surveillance, warning and defence of North America; anti-submarine and coastal patrol; on tactical land support; on SAR and on strategic airlift operations.

Four operational fighter squadrons will be based in Canada — two of them prepared to deploy anywhere in the world on a contingency basis. New helicopters, Arcturus surveillance aircraft and Hercules transports will be added to the inventory. The air force will also continue planning for its eventual participation in space-based surveillance systems.

Like the army, the strength of the Regular air force will drop by about fifteen percent. Reserve enrolment will almost double as the Total Force is applied to the air force as well.

As the numbers and roles assigned to the Reserves expand, so too will the resources devoted to them. For instance: we are currently proceeding with the purchase of the Militia Light Armoured Vehicle and the establishment of regional Militia training centres; an increasing number of Reservists are serving aboard operational fighting ships, and with the acquisition of the coastal patrol vessels, the Naval Reserve will assume additional responsibilities for Maritime defence.

On the issue of the armed forces and the constitutional debate, let me reiterate my remarks from a month ago.

The role of the armed forces will be a silent one.

The Canadian Forces — the most quintessentially national of organizations — remain totally responsive to the federal government and, under circumstances pertaining to law and order, to provincial governments. Other than for purposes of law and order, this country has no history of using the armed forces to resolve domestic disputes. I consider it inconceivable that any duly elected Canadian government would alter that history.

A sense of stability is our most important responsibility and the greatest strength we can give to Canada during the constitutional debate.

In conclusion I would observe that the Canadian Forces are changing to meet a changing world. Traditional enemies are becoming friends, while new dangers emerge. International contingencies are increasingly more difficult to predict.

The CF will continue to play a greater role assisting civil authorities in the protection of Canada's assets. We must be prepared and equipped to fight different kinds of enemies — pollution, drugs and the theft of natural resources also threaten Canadian security.

The focus of Canadian defence policy changed in 1991, but the challenge of service in the Canadian Forces did not.

IX

Strategic Planning and Other Reserve Issues

by
Major General F.A.J. Mariage
Chief of Reserves and Cadets

It gives me great pleasure to be able to tell you today that thanks to the dynamic leadership and continuing support from the CDS and his Commanders, Total Force and the Reserves have made significant strides forward during the past year. The staff efforts which culminated in the formulation of our new defence policy and the ongoing rerolling, restructuring, equipping and facilities improvement programs, as well as the adjustment of personnel policies and procedures to accommodate the reservists and their assignment to operational tasks in growing numbers have had a noticeable effect on the morale of the Reserves.

Yes, there remains much to be done, however, I believe that we are on the way to making Total Force a reality.

Naval Reserve

The Naval Reserve will grow by increments of 101 from 4,212 today to 5,325 in 2002. The future looks good as it is being equipped, trained and tasked as a full-fledged member of the Navy. In keeping with its major role, exercise mines have been acquired, HMCS Moresby and HMCS Anticosti have been equipped with mechanical minesweeping equipment to serve as interim trainer and 12 mine coastal defence vessels will be built and delivered by the end of 1998. As well, Treasury Board has approved the design definition phase of the establishment of the fleet school in Québec City which will be the MCDV, mine warfare and naval control of shipping training centre.

It is obvious that Commander Maritime Command has made the integration of his Reserve a priority and last June I was proud to witness a reservist commanding the ocean safari forces as they made their way into Halifax harbour.

Militia

The militia will grow by increments of 1,300 from 20,105 today to 29,000. Staff action is ongoing to equip the militiaman with a scale of personal weapons, clothing and equipment comparable to his regular counterpart, access to weapons simulators is being secured in training centres across the country and by the end of the decade, 2,400 radios will have been fielded under the tactical command, control and communications program.

The restructuring of the land forces aimed at implementing Total Force is underway. Land Force Central Area (LFCA) and Land Force Western Area (LFWA), which regroup all land forces within a region under a single operational commander, are now a reality. Secteur de l'Est de la Force Terrestre (SEFT) will follow this year; Land Force Atlantic Area (LFAA) and Land Force Northern Area (LFNA) will follow shortly after to complete the regional structure. It is expected that this restructuring will do much to fully integrate the militia into the regular army.

I am also happy to inform you that the militia concentrations were attended in record numbers this past summer and that the militia has continued to contribute to FMC's operational tasks in increasing numbers. Reservists have been assigned to Cyprus, Kuwait, Goose Bay and to other tasks where they have acquitted themselves splendidly. This is an indication not only of the increased level of training of the militia but also of their importance in terms of sharing the load with the regulars. FMC, with support from my branch, is investigating a ready reserve concept in order to reinforce the Total Force.

These increased numbers and their increasing participation in operational tasks have strained the militia's budget but with the strong support of the CDS, additional funds were made available and the militia should finish the year in good condition.

I am confident that with the steps already taken and those contemplated by Commander FMC, the land forces are on their way to Total Force.

Air Reserve

The Air Reserve will grow from 1,594 to 2,016 in 1995 and to more than 3,000 in 2002.

Dynamic leadership and a strong emphasis on total integration of the Air Reserve personnel and units into the regular Air Force training and operations have created a success story. The principle of common usage of equipment has been adopted and, as a result, the Air Reserve units are being rerolled to fly the same aircraft as the regulars. Personnel are being integrated into all squadrons, flying all types of aircraft with a commensurate increase in their state of readiness and morale. I worked with General Huddleston when he was DCDS and have no doubt about his intention to carry Total Force through.

Communications Reserve

The Communications Reserve will grow from 2,135 today to 3,559 by 2002.

Commander CFCC's training and employment policies for his reserve has made Total Force a reality in that Command for a number of years already. Indeed, that Command has been and continues to be the leader in Total Force issues. Currently, the main thrust of the Communications Reserve is the integration of units in which regular force personnel as well as some regular force detachments are under command of reserve units. Under development is a Total Force communications unit in which some 70% of its 800 personnel will consist of reservists.

Just last week, I was again impressed with the enthusiasm and dedication of communication reservists as I was visiting 744 COMMS regiment in Vancouver.

Rangers

The Ranger Programme is in its initial phase of expansion with Pacific Region being reactivated with 190 Rangers as of this month. The Rangers presently total 2,367 and this will be increased to about 3,000 by 1995. The Rangers continue to impress me with their eagerness to join the program and their pride in being part of the team. Along with their expansion, the Rangers are the object of a strategic study which will rationalize their training and roles.

Last week, with the approval of the CDS, I had the privilege of launching Exercise Baton Ranger where the Rangers, whose area of operation borders our three oceans, were given a mission befitting that fact. They were given the mission to relay a baton from Vancouver Island, up the Pacific coast, across the north, down the Atlantic coast to Newfoundland where they are to deliver that baton, along with the log depicting its journey, as a celebration of the 50th anniversary of the formation of the Pacific Coast Militia Rangers and of the 125th anniversary of our confederation. I have no doubt that they will acquit themselves well.

Pan-Reserve Issues

In terms of pan-reserve issues, there have been a number of developments during the past year.

RIPT

The Reserve Integration Planning Team, an ADM (Personnel) sponsored initiative aimed at examining personnel policies and procedures with a view to adapting them to the Total Force, has completed their study and has recommended changes to more than 100 personnel policies. The majority of these are in various stages of implementation.

RPPS

The Reserve Personnel and Pay System, which is to replace the present antiquated system, is the single most important factor in the day to day administration of the Reserves. Some of you may be aware that the contractor is having major problems with the system's software. This is being resolved and the system should be in operation next fall.

RIIP

The Reserve Integrated Information Project is the successor of the Reserve Personnel and Pay System and is scheduled for implementation in the second part of the decade. Its aim is to increase the operational effectiveness of the integrated reserve force by providing a responsive automated information system to support administration, training and logistic activities of the reserves and to support the mobilization process in times of peace, emergencies and war. This project is receiving the necessary approval at its different stages of development and is proceeding on schedule.

Benefits

Health benefits and the Reserve Term Insurance Plan, which are similar in benefits and costs to that of the regular force, have been almost fully implemented and will be in place to provide administrative support to the RRPS when it becomes operational.

The Reserve Force Retirement Allowance, which is identical to that of the Regular Force, is expected to be approved very shortly and to take effect in April 1993 when Bill C-29, which also applies to the Canadian Forces, allows changes to compensation plans for the public service.

Pay Comparability

A great deal of staff effort has also been dedicated to pay comparability. Approval in principle has been received for a new methodology to compare regular and reserve pay structures. While this method will narrow the gap, it is still too early to confirm when it will be implemented.

Armouries

Many of our armouries and naval reserve divisions need to be replaced or renovated, and additional armouries must be constructed. The long term plan aimed at constructing, refurbishing or leasing four armouries or divisions per year was implemented in 1987 and will continue to address the shortfalls.

Strategic plan

I have now held my appointment for over a year. Among other things, I have utilized that time to gain fresh insights into the state of the Reserves and the direction that strategic change is taking us. We are very encouraged by the evidence of positive accomplishments made on a variety of key issues, which ultimately impact not only on the general effectiveness of the Reserves but also the perception of their value to our overall defence commitments.

We note, however, that although we see ourselves making tactical gains on a wide front, we have yet to be able to tie together all of the activities in one major plan or concept. The current reality is that the reserve component will be required to play a more substantive role in the defence and security of the country, within the Total Force. Since that is irrefutable, we believe that we need a road map for the future of the Reserves. With this in mind, we in the branch have developed a strategic plan to enable us to more effectively support ongoing initiatives and to ensure that our branch's activities are complementary to developing issues in other branches, groups and the commands, and also provide a measuring stick for the CDS.

Approach

To formulate this plan, we first established our aim for the Reserves which is "to have an effective reserve component, within a viable Total Force, which enables the Canadian Forces to carry out its assigned defence and security responsibilities in peacetime and emergencies or war."

We then analyzed the characteristics of the reserve component — recognizing that reservists are citizens who train on a part-time basis with strengths and limitations different from their regular force counterparts. We concluded that for the reserve component to be effective within the Total Force it should have the following characteristics:

1. Must be a reflection of and have the support of Canadian society at large;
2. Must be competently led and highly motivated;
3. Must be individually and collectively trained to standards appropriate to their operational readiness requirements;
4. Must be structured to facilitate command, control, administration and training in peacetime with a capacity for expansion and sustainment during emergencies and war;
5. They must be supported by the necessary numbers of full-time personnel assisting with administration, training and operational requirements;
6. They must be funded to recruit, train and retrain sufficient personnel to support their required role within Total Force;
7. They must be appropriately equipped to meet training and operational requirements;
8. They must have job protection through voluntary and/or legislated employer support for training, emergencies or war; and

9. There must be mutual respect, confidence and support on behalf of both regular and reserve components.

We analyzed these desirable characteristics, looking at the strengths and weaknesses of our reserves at this moment in time. We naturally noted that there are many ongoing initiatives within the Canadian Forces and that many of these areas are largely within the purview of the Commands. We still, however, examined each of these desirable characteristics in detail to judge the impact on, and involvement of, our branch. In some of these areas, we are clearly the lead agency.

Strategic plan

From our analysis, we developed our branch strategic plan. We set goals, objectives and specific responsibilities for the staff, and we now have in place a means by which we can get a feel for our progress, and more easily spot those areas in which we should concentrate our efforts. We can also see where we might best support command initiatives and activities. It will be through the environmental and command staffs on a day-to-day basis that we take formal action, and through our informal contacts with the senior reserve advisors, as well as through the Reserve Council, and from you, that we can get further advice and assistance.

Twice yearly the Chief of Reserves and Cadets will report to the Armed Forces Council on those activities within his purview, and with its members support perhaps we can give the CDS a more global view on the state of affairs of the reserve component.

Strategic Plan For the National Employer Support Committee

A characteristic of particular significance is that the reserve component must have job protection through voluntary or legislated employer support. A 1988 study concluded that while job protection could be legislated for war or crisis situations, it was not advisable for peacetime training, at least until other methods had been explored, and that it was preferable to enlist the employer's "voluntary support".

It is not necessary to elaborate to this group the rationale which led to the conclusion that employer support would have to be sought much more aggressively in the future. Suffice it to say that based on the statement made by the Minister of National Defence, in September:

— the growth of the reserve component is such that it will come to represent 34% of the Total Force, up nine percentage points from the current 25%;

— in the case of the land force, which will represent 65% of the Total Force, a total of 60% will consist of reservists; and

— the changes in the numbers and the implementation of the Total Force concept will result in increased roles and responsibilities for reserves, of which more than a third are currently employed.

The decision was reached, therefore, to revitalize NESC and to provide incentives for employer support. In order to achieve these goals, the role of the NESC was redefined: "to promote the Canadian Reserve Forces through trade associations, small and large businesses, government and municipal agencies, etc. . . . In order to facilitate the hiring of reservists and the granting of leave of absence for training without loss in job promotion and vacation time".

Because employer support was recognized as such a priority and due to the interest shown in the past by CDA in the matter, I thought that it would be desirable to give you more information on the strategy which will be used by the NESC.

The employer support program falls within my area of responsibility. The Chairman of the Committee is John Craig Eaton, the President of Eaton's of Canada. The Chairman is appointed by the Minister of National Defence, and is assisted by two vice-chairmen, one for the east and one for the west; there is also a chairman in each province.

Secondly, we are in the process of establishing a network of military representatives, who will act as provincial liaison officers. Finally, the work of NESC is coordinated by a small office at NDHQ, headed by a new Executive Director, Léo M. Desmarteau. It gives me great pleasure now to introduce to you the Chairman of the NESC who, having already made a significant contribution to the support of the Reserves, has agreed to take on the new and monumental challenges now facing the NESC.

Remarks by Mr. Eaton

Thank you for the opportunity to share with you some thoughts on the work of the NESC.

I do not need to describe to you in detail that this is not the best of times, economically speaking, to approach employers and request their support of the Canadian Forces. Employers can appreciate our motive to increase the cost effectiveness of the military. But we must not give employers the impression that those who employ and support reservists are in effect subsidizing the Canadian Forces and not getting anything in return.

The NESC has decided on a new way to relate to employers. Instead of approaching them with a request for two weeks of military leave and full pay, we will approach them with an offer; hopefully an offer they can't refuse. We will offer the reservist as a more productive employee.

The training provided by the Canadian Forces already enjoys an enviable reputation among employers; it is then up to us to demonstrate the benefits of military training to the employers of reservists. In return for this contribution to their productivity, we may ask for the employer's support.

While this strategy is likely to yield positive results, it likely will not be sufficient to cover the new requirements with regard to the roles and responsibilities of the Reserves. In order to ensure increased availability of reservists for tasking, training and other functions, it may prove necessary for the military and employers to discuss new cooperative arrangements. In some cases a partnership between the military and employers will be the way to ensure the required flexibility on both sides of the offer.

The NESC is in a position to create an environment which will be conducive to the achievement of results which will be beneficial to both the Canadian Forces and employers. And I can assure you that the 15 members of the NESC will continue to pursue that objective relentlessly.

I would now like to call upon the Executive Director of NESC to explain to us how he will accomplish all this.

Remarks by Mr. Léo Desmarteau

The translation of the basic strategy into an action plan, or an operation, calls for a marketing approach. Basically, the reservist is the product and employers are the consumers of that product.

We will undertake to describe the product, in terms of trades training, transferrable skills and values, such as leadership, teamwork, discipline, loyalty, time management, organizational skills, etc. These qualifications will be stated in terms of factors of productivity.

The consumers will be defined as target groups and they will be approached systematically. Such groups would be, for example:

— current employers of reservists;
— defence industries;
— the three levels of government and related agencies;
— industries and businesses regrouped by trade or sectors; and
— associations and organizations.

The assistance of various groups and organizations will be sought, such as the military, unions, politicians, etc. The NESC message will be given through publications, promotional material, mailings, visits to military exercises, speeches, conference booths, etc. The employers will be presented with a description of the benefits of employing reservists and what is expected from them. Activities to improve the relationship between the Reserves and employers will be carried out by the units, at the local level, at the provincial level and at the national level.

In closing, I would like to ask you to forgive me for my boldness, as I would like to issue a challenge to this audience.

Assuming that all of you know our product very well and considering that a large percentage of the people in this room are employers or senior employees, I am wondering how many would be prepared to try and have their company adopt a policy of support for the Reserves. May I ask that anyone interested in considering this possibility give me your business card, so that I may send you some related material.

Conclusion by Major General Mariage

I believe that we are at a milestone in the evolution of our reserve component. We have the new defence policy paper, we have the many, but sometimes disconnected, initiatives through the past four years. We are undergoing the Auditor General's comprehensive audit of the reserve component, and we have an increasing requirement, if not necessity, for the Reserves to play a more significant role within the Total Force of the future. We must also get the military in greater contact with mainstream Canada. It is therefore all the more important that our branch have a strategic plan which ensures that our efforts help tie together and support the many ongoing activities, and take advantage of new opportunities. And, hopefully we can tie together all reserve plans and initiatives to concentrate our efforts, reinforce our strengths, accommodate inherent limitations, and achieve the long term goals and objectives of the Total Force.

With this strategic plan as a foundation, my branch has developed specific goals, objectives and tasking. However one must remember that my branch does not command the Reserves, it exists only to advise on or help initiate and develop policy. If the strategic plan is to work then it must be adopted and given support outside the branch. For example, different levels of command can support its implementation:

a. NDHQ — influences personnel policies, force structure, mobilization planning, capital and equipment decisions, and, of course, money;

b. Commands — training reserves and dealing with force structure in detail;

c. Area, district, or reserve element HQ — more emphasis on leadership (e.g. career management of reserves), training, and developing a good rapport between the regular and the reserve force;

d. Unit CO's — recruiting, training, and motivating their reservists; and

e. Honoraries, associations, and others — your involvement is a matter of your particular scope of interest and you should take on those matters you could best assist us with.

It must be stressed that all these levels must develop their own specific strategic plan, based on the more general C Res and Cdts strategic plan, in order to bring about the necessary positive and coordinated changes.

And this enables me to throw a second challenge to you. Develop your own plan in support of this strategic plan, and let me know about it by next Easter.

The initiative in progress will change the nature of the Reserves. They will result in Reserves that are more effective, more capable and more useful. The Reserves will be better integrated into the Total Force, and Total Force will be a better reflection of Canadian society.

For our Reserves of the future we believe that the key to success lies in the improvement of operational training; on the rationalization of our organizational structures, our standards and equipment scales etc., and particularly on the intimate and constant support of the regular force.